WILLIAMS
SONOMA
CALIFORNIA

BAKING

FAVORITES

RECIPES BY

**WILLIAMS SONOMA
TEST KITCHEN**

weldon**owen**

CONTENTS

INTRODUCTION

What could be more enticing than the aroma of freshly baked goods coming from the oven? Baking evokes so many wonderful emotions, filling your kitchen with the memories of childhood, the nostalgia of the holidays, and the everyday joy of creating and sharing homemade treats. The only thing that's better is the first bite of a warm chocolate chip cookie, a flaky piecrust filled with juicy peaches, or a lemony loaf cake flecked with poppy seeds. The more than 100 recipes collected here provide delicious inspiration for any occasion throughout the year.

For some home bakers, even the simplest recipes can seem intimidating, so we're here to help you master the basics. From prepping pans and whipping up airy batters to proofing, baking, and decorating your masterpieces, this book will guide you through invaluable baking how-tos. You'll find an overview of ingredients and essential tools, decorating techniques, and troubleshooting tips to help ensure sweet success every time.

With these building blocks in hand, you'll be all set to bake our favorite sweet and savory recipes for ultimate classics and modern specialties—they'll inspire your creativity and evoke "oohs" and "aahs" from friends and family. A colorful array of spritz cookies, a decadent bûche de Noël, or a tender vegetable potpie are just right for cozy winter holidays. Celebrate summer with a crusty plum galette, zesty lemon bars, or a crumbly strawberry-rhubarb pie. And for a delectable accompaniment to any gathering, try chewy everything bagels, gluten-free skillet cornbread, or warm, fluffy cinnamon rolls with cream cheese frosting.

No matter how you bake it, decorate it, or serve it, there's a homemade treat for every season, every event, and every taste in the pages ahead.

ESSENTIAL BAKING INGREDIENTS

Most recipes use a similar stockpile of ingredients: butter, flour, sugar, eggs, and vanilla or other flavorings. Using the highest quality of each yields the best results. Unless otherwise directed, use room-temperature ingredients, as they blend easily and result in a fluffier texture.

FLOUR

Many recipes in this book are made using all-purpose flour or cake flour. All-purpose flour is better both for sturdier cakes that require the structure provided by the small amount of gluten it contains, and for pies, which require little to no gluten development in order to achieve a tender, flaky crust. Lighter, more delicate cakes and brownies require finely milled cake flour, which is lower in protein and gluten. If you'd like, you can substitute 1 cup (4 oz/125 g) plus 2 tablespoons cake flour for every 1 cup (5 oz/155 g) all-purpose flour.

Alternative flours, like almond flour, are ideal when making cake decorations using marzipan, making tortes and flourless cakes, and for gluten-free pie doughs.

SUGAR

In its various forms, sugar lends both sweetness and moisture and, when it caramelizes in the oven, gives baked goods a deliciously golden hue. White granulated sugar, light brown sugar, and confectioners' sugar—also called powdered sugar—are the most common types used in this book.

BUTTER & OIL

Butter and oil deliver moisture, tenderness, and flavor to baked goods. Choose a flavorless oil, such as canola or vegetable oil, unless otherwise specified. Use unsalted butter because it allows you to control the amount of salt added and lends a sweeter flavor to your treats. When whipped with sugar, butter keeps the crumb light and airy and even helps leaven cakes. When beaten into sweet meringue or with confectioners' sugar and other flavorings, butter creates silky rich frostings and buttercreams.

The temperature of the butter is important: if the butter is too cold, it will not fluff up or cream properly, and if it is too warm or nearly melted, it will be too thin to fluff up at all. If the temperature of the butter is not specified, opt for room-temperature butter for best results.

EGGS

The egg is one of the most versatile ingredients in the baker's kitchen. Whipped egg whites add air and leavening to many batters, create the airy texture of meringues and pavlovas, serve as the base for royal icing used in cookie decorating, and can be transformed into a meringue topping and base for buttercream. Egg yolks are ideal for adding richness and for creating curds and custards. Whole eggs lend structure to any baked good. The recipes in this book call for large eggs. For the freshest results, choose organic, pasture-raised eggs.

DAIRY

Dairy products like milk, buttermilk, and sour cream add richness, flavor, fat, and moisture to baked goods. The recipes in this book use whole milk and full-fat sour cream for the best flavor. If you don't have buttermilk or sour cream, use plain whole-milk yogurt.

BAKING SODA & BAKING POWDER

Leavening is the result of gas bubbles expanding in batters and doughs as they bake, causing the baked good to rise and lightening the texture and crumb. While some cake and cookie recipes are leavened purely with whipped egg whites, other recipes include chemical leaveners, such as baking soda and baking powder. Baking soda must be used with another acidic ingredient in the batter, such as sour cream or lemon juice; it is activated when mixed with wet ingredients. Baking powder is a mixture of baking soda and a dry acid, like cream of tartar, and a little cornstarch. It's usually "double acting," meaning it is activated by both moisture and heat. You can substitute baking powder for baking soda but not vice versa.

FLAVORINGS

Chocolate and cocoa powder, vanilla extract or vanilla beans, citrus zest, liqueurs and other extracts, and countless spices like cinnamon and nutmeg can help shape the personality of your finished creation.

BAKING EQUIPMENT & TOOLS

Using the right tools ensures the best results and gives your baked goods a polished appearance. Here are the indispensable tools that help you beat batters and doughs easily, whip up the fluffiest frostings, and create professional-style decorations.

ELECTRIC MIXER

An electric stand mixer will help you make batters, doughs, fillings, and frostings with ease. While some batters can be prepared with just a bowl and a wooden spoon or a handheld whisk, you'll find it far easier to whip egg whites and whole eggs and to cream butter and sugar with a sturdy tabletop mixer. There are two commonly used attachments for a stand mixer: the paddle, also called the flat beater, which is ideal for creaming butter and sugar and beating batters and doughs, and the whisk, or whip, attachment, which aerates egg whites, whole eggs, and cream. Handheld mixers will also work, although they lack the power of a stand mixer and often cannot beat thick or sturdy mixtures.

FOOD PROCESSOR

We recommend making pie dough in a food processor using a standard blade or a dough blade. The dough comes together quickly, and you don't risk warming up the dough with your hands. A food processor is also handy for finely grinding ingredients such as nuts, pretzels, and graham crackers.

If you don't have a food processor, you can make pie dough by hand using a pastry blender or two table knives. For crushing or grinding ingredients, place them in a resealable plastic bag, lock the top while letting out the air, and crush the ingredients to their desired size using a rolling pin.

ROLLING PINS

A wooden pin with a heavy cylinder that rolls independently of its two handles works well with sturdy pie and cookie doughs, but there are numerous types available. A rolling pin is also used when working with marzipan for cake decorating.

SIFTER

Sifting dry ingredients, such as flour, baking powder or baking soda, cocoa, and confectioners' sugar, lightens them so that they don't deflate the whipped ingredients they're being folded into. Sifting also removes any lumps, particularly in fine dry ingredients that tend to clump, including cake flour, cocoa, and confectioners' sugar. Choose a fine-mesh sifter or sieve for best results.

SPATULAS

A heatproof silicone rubber spatula is great for stirring batter, scraping it out of the bowl and into the pan, and spreading it evenly before baking. An offset spatula, which features a stiff metal blade that is bent near the handle, facilitates moving cake layers from wire cooling racks to a cake stand or platter, and is useful for spreading fillings, frostings, and glazes. An icing spatula has a long, straight blade and is also excellent for spreading fillings, frostings, and glazes.

CUTTERS

A paring knife, pizza wheel, and/or kitchen shears are all helpful when trimming excess dough from a lined pie dish or cutting out strips of dough (with the help of a ruler) for a lattice top.

DOUGH SCRAPER

When rolling out the dough, it's important that it doesn't stick to the work surface. A dusting of flour helps, but to easily move the dough around and to loosen it when it does stick, a scraper works wonders.

COOKIE PRESS

You'll need a cookie press for our Spritz Cookies (page 25) and a special madeleine pan for Chuck Williams' own recipe for madeleines (page 38).

PARCHMENT PAPER

Use parchment paper or silicone baking mats to line baking sheets to prevent dough from sticking.

BAKING SHEETS

Baking sheets are used for baking cookies, focaccia, and sheet cakes. Cookies can be baked on either rimmed or rimless baking sheets lined with parchment paper or silicone baking mats to prevent dough from sticking. Sheet cakes and roulades, or rolled cakes, are typically baked in a 12-by-16-inch (30-by-40-cm) sheet cake pan (also called a half sheet pan or rimmed baking sheet) with 1-inch (2.5-cm) sides.

PIE WEIGHTS

When partially or fully baking a pie shell before filling it (see page 233), you will need pie weights to help the crust hold its shape during baking. You can purchase ceramic pie weights (which look like small balls), or use dried beans or uncooked rice.

PIE DISHES

A standard-sized pie dish is 9 inches (23 cm) in diameter and 1½ inches (4 cm) deep and is used for most of the pies in this cookbook. Some recipes require a deep-dish pie dish, which is 2–4 inches (5–10 cm) deep. Pie dishes are made of glass, metal, or ceramic. Glass conducts heat particularly well, plus it allows you to see if the bottom of the crust is nicely browned. If using a metal pie dish, choose a thick, sturdy steel one.

CAKE PANS

Different cakes require different types and sizes of pans. Whatever pan you use, be sure to prep it as directed in your recipe before making the batter, as it will need to go in the oven immediately. For most cake pans, choose ones made from sturdy, heavy-duty aluminum.

Round cake pans: Most of the layer cake recipes in this book call for two round 8- or 9-inch (20- to 23-cm) cake pans that are 2 inches (5 cm) high. Avoid nonstick pans when baking sponge cakes, which need an ungreased surface in order to rise high.

Muffin pans: Standard-sized or mini, a muffin pan can be greased or lined with paper cupcake liners for cupcakes, tea cakes, and other mini or bite-sized cakes.

Specialty pans: Angel food and chiffon cakes are traditionally made in a tall, 10-inch (25-cm) diameter footed tube pan with a removable base. A Bundt pan is a popular ring-shaped pan that gives cakes a distinctive scalloped or patterned look; they range in size from mini to extra large, but 12-cup (3-l) pans are the most common. A springform pan features a spring-loaded latch that tightens a collar around a removable base; these are great for tall cakes, coffee cakes, and cheesecakes.

PASTRY BAGS & TIPS

Made from washable canvas, silicone, or plastic, a pastry bag is useful when dividing small amounts of batter, piping filling on a layer of cake, and putting the final decorative touches on your masterpiece. A set of plain and star tips will enable you to frost and decorate with professional finesse.

GENERAL BAKING TIPS

From mixing batters and making doughs to storing them properly, different baked goods require different methods. Here are our tips and techniques for achieving the best results with your baking.

WORKING WITH BATTER

When creating a cake batter, use these pointers to prevent a heavy, dense cake or a cake with large air pockets. For other types of batters, such as brownies, read the recipe directions carefully as these tips may not apply.

Folding in Ingredients

- To fold whipped egg whites (or whipped cream) into a batter, you want to retain as much aeration as possible, so use a gentle hand and as few strokes as possible.

- With a large rubber spatula, dollop a scoop of the whipped egg whites onto the batter, then gently stir it in; this step lightens the batter to make it easier for folding. Spoon the remaining egg whites onto the batter.

- Starting in the center of the bowl, use the rubber spatula to "slice" through the whites and batter to the bottom of the bowl, then pull the spatula up the side of the bowl and swoop over the top and back to the middle. This action will gently mix the egg whites and batter together.

- Continue with this motion, rotating the bowl, until the mixture is combined and no white streaks are visible, being careful not to overmix and lose the aeration.

Mixing Batter

- To prevent overmixing, stop mixing just when you see that the ingredients are evenly blended and you can no longer see streaks of individual ingredients.

- If you see streaks of ingredients like flour or baking powder in your batter, be sure that you mix the ingredients thoroughly until evenly blended to prevent undermixing.

WORKING WITH DOUGH

Depending on what you're baking, different doughs will have different textures, visual cues, a different methods of handling. These expert how-tos prevent results that are dense, tough, or chewy.

COOKIE DOUGH

The first few times you work with cookie dough can be tricky. But like other rewarding baking adventures, practice makes perfect—especially if you follow these handy tips.

Rolling out Dough

- Flour your work surface and rolling pin before getting started. Or, if the dough becomes too sticky and tricky, roll it between sheets of waxed or parchment paper.

- When rolling out dough, work quickly so that it doesn't become too warm. This will help ensure that the cutout shapes don't spread when they bake. If your kitchen is warm, refrigerate the cutout cookies on a baking sheet for 15 to 20 minutes before putting them in the oven.

Cutting Dough

- Dip cookie cutters in flour before pressing them into the dough, and place cookie cutters close to the edge of the rolled-out dough so you can cut out as many cookies as possible and minimize scraps.

- If you can't find the right cookie cutter, trace the shape out with scissors. Then place this template directly on the rolled-out dough and cut out shapes with the tip of a paring knife.

- For special occasions, make a big impact by using cookie cutters in the same shape but in an assortment of sizes. Try this with Gingerbread Cookies (page 45) during the holidays. Be sure to group similar sizes together on separate sheets so they bake evenly.

- If dough scraps become sticky, refrigerate them for 10 minutes before rerolling. (And resist the temptation to roll the same piece of dough more than twice.)

Freezing Dough

- For best results, follow the instructions in each recipe regarding chilling and wrapping cookie dough; many require refrigerating the dough for at least 1 hour or up to overnight.

- To save time, the dough for some recipes can be prepared ahead and then frozen, as with the Sugar Cookies (page 210). If working with frozen dough, let it stand at room temperature for a few minutes before shaping or slicing.

- Rolled cookie dough should never get too warm or it will spread while baking. When making Spritz Cookies (page 25), be sure that the dough is at room temperature as it needs to be soft enough to extrude easily from the cookie press.

PIE DOUGH

To make the pie dough gluten-free, simply use the Gluten-Free Dough (page 213) in any recipe that calls for Basic Pie Dough. For gluten-based dough, it's important to not develop the gluten in the dough to avoid a flat, tough crust. Here are tried-and-true tips to guarantee success every time.

Working with Ingredients

- Use very cold ingredients; butter should be straight from the refrigerator.

- Be sure the butter is unsalted.

- Use very cold water (or other liquid, depending on the recipe). Combine ice and water in a measuring cup and then measure the water from that, avoiding the ice.

- Use a food processor to mix the dough to keep your warm hands off of the dough.

Creating Dough

- Be careful not to overmix the dough; just pulse the ingredients in the processor.

- Cut the butter into cubes, then add it to the dry ingredients in the processor and pulse just until the butter is the size of peas.

- Add the ice water and pulse just until the liquid is evenly dispersed. The dough will look crumbly, but it should come together when pressed firmly. If it crumbles, add more ice water, a tablespoonful at a time, and pulse just until the dough holds together when pinched.

Shaping Dough

- Dump the dough onto a well-floured work surface and press it into a disk.

- Wrap the dough in plastic wrap.

- Chill the dough in the refrigerator for at least 30 minutes before using.

BREAD DOUGH

Baking bread may seem intimidating to those who have little to no experience, but anyone with a few minutes to spare can make homemade bread a dinner-table staple! Breadmaking is all about developing the gluten; use these tips as your guide to creating the perfect loaf.

Working with Ingredients

- Work with organic, high-quality ingredients whenever possible to achieve a well-risen loaf.

- Use a digital kitchen scale for measuring ingredients whenever possible. Small amounts of less than 10g should be measured using measuring spoons.

Creating Dough

- A well-kneaded dough should look smooth and feel slightly tacky to the touch.

- To test whether the dough is ready for the oven, poke it with your finger. The dough should spring back slowly and still have a small indentation. If it springs back quickly, let it rise for a few minutes longer.

BAKE LIKE A PRO

Because baking is a science, trial-and-error is a common method for becoming a better baker. Use our primer as both a preventative measure and as a troubleshooting guide to achieve success with your baked goods—and to work around common challenges.

CAKES

Sometimes, despite our best efforts, a cake simply doesn't turn out in the way we would like. Here are some of the most common problems we encountered when testing the recipes for this book, and the best ways to solve them so your next cake will bake to perfection.

Before & During Baking

- Once you spread the batter in the cake pan, gently tap the pan on the counter to release any air pockets. Alternatively, drag a wooden skewer through the batter.

- To prevent a burnt top, loosely drape aluminum foil over the top of the cake if it begins to overbrown during baking.

- If your cake isn't rising in the oven, make sure that you added the leavening or that it isn't out of date.

After Baking

- If the cake overbrowns despite your best efforts, use a long serrated knife to trim the burnt area from the top of the cake and discard.

- If the cake shrinks from the pan sides during baking, this may be the result of a number of factors:

  - Overmixing the batter—be careful not to overmix the batter, especially when folding in aerated ingredients.

  - Too much leavener—be sure to use level teaspoons, not heaping ones.

- Inaccurate oven temperature—check temperature with an oven thermometer, and take care not to overbake the cake.

- Overgreasing the pan—a thin layer of butter or cooking oil spray, and sometimes another of flour, helps prevent cakes from sticking to the pan.

- If the cake comes out lumpy or contains streaks of ingredients, the cake batter may have been undermixed.

- If the cake comes out heavy or dense, the cake batter may have been overmixed.

- Don't toss out a misshapen or poorly risen cake! Cut it into chunks and use it for a trifle (a layered dessert with cake, sherry, custard, fruit, and whipped cream).

Storing Cakes

- To store an uncut and unfrosted cake, wrap the cake tightly in plastic wrap so that the plastic is touching the top, sides, and bottom. The cake can be stored at room temperature for 2–3 days.

- To store a frosted but uncut cake, cover the cake with a cake dome or a large bowl and store at room temperature for 2–3 days.

- To store a frosted and cut cake, press a piece of plastic wrap against the cut area, then cover with a cake dome or large bowl and store at room temperature for 2–3 days.

COOKIES

Cookie dough and finished cookies are delicate. It is important to handle cookies with care at every stage of the process—from prepping, rolling, and cutting to cooling, decorating, and storing.

Before & During Baking

- Oven temperatures vary, and since cookies have short baking times, it is important to watch them closely so they don't burn. Check for doneness a couple of minutes before the recipe indicates.

- To ensure even cooking, rotate the baking sheets halfway through the baking time.

- Use wire racks for cooling; they allow air to circulate beneath the cookies, which helps them cool quickly and evenly.

- When making bar cookies, use the size of dish called for in the recipe—using a different size will change the baking time and may affect the texture.

After Baking

- If the cookies spread too much during baking, the butter was too soft when added, or the dough was placed on a hot baking sheet.

- If the cookies are burned on the bottom, the cookies were too thin, the oven was too hot, the baking sheet was too thin or placed too low in the oven, or the baking sheets were not rotated during baking.

- If the cookies did not bake evenly, the baking sheets were not rotated during baking.

- If the cookies fell apart when removed from the baking sheet, the cookies were removed from the baking sheet too soon.

- If the cookies stuck to the baking sheet, the cookies were not baked long enough or were left too long on the baking sheet.

Storing Cookies

- Most cookies will keep well in an airtight container, layered between sheets of parchment paper, at room temperature for a few days.

- To pack bar treats for picnics and parties, wrap them individually in aluminum foil or waxed paper.

- A dozen beautifully baked cookies can easily become the perfect hostess or holiday gift. Wrap cookies in waxed paper and place on colorful tissue paper in a sturdy decorative box or metal tin, then tie with festive ribbon.

PIES

Pie doughs are half the battle when it comes to making a perfect pie. Luckily, a perfect filling and a tender crust are easy to achieve with a little practice and mindful preparation.

Before & During Baking

- Always chill your dough before baking to prevent a tough crust.

- Choose fresh, ripe, in-season fruit for the best flavor and texture in fillings.

- Depending on the sweetness and juiciness of the fruit, as well as your own palate, adjust the amount of sugar you add—more for unripe or less-flavorful fruit and less for very ripe, sweet fruit.

- Fruit pies need thickeners so they aren't runny. Cornstarch is our preferred thickener in this cookbook, especially for summer fruits. Potato starch or tapioca starch are also excellent options.

- For double-crust and lattice-topped pies, brush the top of the dough with an egg wash, a mixture of one large egg beaten with about 1 teaspoon water for a shiny, golden brown crust that helps turbinado sugar or other finishing toppings to adhere to the crust.

- If the edges of the pie are overbrowning in the oven, cut strips of aluminum foil and crimp them over the edges of the crust as the pie finishes baking.

After Baking

- If the pie falls apart or is excessively juicy, the pie was cut too soon. Fruit pies need to cool for at least four hours before serving, while custard pies need at least two hours in the refrigerator before serving. Savory pies are designed to be eaten hot or warm.

- If the piecrust isn't flaky or is tough, the ingredients used were too warm, the dough itself was too warm or was not chilled before baking, or the butter and dough were overworked.

- If the bottom crust is soggy, the oven temperature was too low, the oven rack was too high and the crust did not get enough heat, or the pie was not cooled on a wire rack, preventing air from circulating under it.

Storing Pies

- To store custard pies or pies with egg or dairy in the filling, cover with plastic wrap and store in the refrigerator for up to 4 days.

- To store fruit pies, cover with aluminum foil and store at room temperature for up to 2 days or in the refrigerator for up to 5 days.

BREAD

Regardless of whether you're a baking pro or just starting out, baking bread is a skill that can easily elevate your meals. For more specific information regarding sourdough bread and sourdough starters, see page 194.

Before & During Baking

- You'll want to make your sourdough starter about 1–2 weeks before you plan on baking the loaf.

- For sourdough breads, always make sure you feed your starter consistently at the same time each day.

- Resting and baking times are approximate and depend on the temperature of the kitchen and the temperature of the oven, respectively. Visual cues will be important for determining whether your dough or loaf is ready.

- To achieve the crunchy crust of focaccia, drizzle a generous amount of olive oil over the bread before, during, and after baking.

After Baking

- With the exception of flatbreads and rolls, bread fresh out of the oven will continue to cook as they cool. For best results in taste and texture, let your loaf cool to room temperature before slicing.

- If your crust looks and feels crispy out of the oven but softens as it cools or has a dense interior when cut, the bread may be underbaked. Check your oven temperature and allow your bread to fully cool before cutting. If the problem persists, you may need to decrease the amount of liquid used.

- If your bread is dry, it may be overbaked. If your oven temperature is accurate, you may need to use less flour when kneading or working with the dough.

Storing Bread

- Unlike store-bought breads, which contain preservatives, fresh bread will spoil quicker.

- Bread may be stored in an airtight container at room temperature for up to 7 days.

- If your bread dries out, don't throw it away! Stale bread is great for making French toast, bread pudding, and croutons.

COOKIES, BARS & BROWNIES

Snickerdoodles

When you bake these sweet treats, your kitchen will fill with the heady aroma of cinnamon. The best versions of this sugar-cookie relative emerge deliciously chewy once cooled and are perfect for dipping into a glass of cold milk.

2¾ cups (11 oz/310 g) all-purpose flour

2 teaspoons cream of tartar

1 teaspoon baking soda

½ teaspoon kosher salt

1 cup (8 oz/225 g) unsalted butter, at room temperature

1½ cups (10½ oz/300 g) plus ⅓ cup (2½ oz/70 g) sugar

1 teaspoon pure vanilla extract

2 large eggs

2½ tablespoons ground cinnamon

MAKES ABOUT 2 DOZEN COOKIES

Place 1 rack in the upper third and 1 rack in the lower third of the oven and preheat the oven to 400°F (200°C). Line 2 baking sheets with parchment paper.

In a bowl, sift together the flour, cream of tartar, baking soda, and salt. Set aside.

In the bowl of a stand mixer fitted with the paddle attachment, beat the butter on medium speed until smooth, about 2 minutes. Add the 1½ cups (10½ oz/300 g) sugar and beat until light and fluffy, about 2 minutes. Add the vanilla and add the eggs one at a time, beating well after each addition. Stop the mixer and scrape down the sides of the bowl. Add the flour mixture and beat on low speed until just combined, about 1 minute.

In a small bowl, stir together the ⅓ cup (2½ oz/70 g) sugar and the cinnamon. Shape the dough into 1½-inch (4-cm) balls and roll in the cinnamon-sugar mixture to coat. Place on the prepared baking sheets, spacing the cookies about 2 inches (5 cm) apart.

Bake until the cookies are slightly cracked on top and puffed up, about 10 minutes, rotating the baking sheets between the racks halfway through baking.

Let cool on baking sheets for 5 minutes, then transfer to a wire rack to cool completely, or serve warm.

Spritz Cookies

You will need a cookie press to make these crisp, buttery cookies, a favorite of German bakers at Christmastime. The best presses include a wide selection of plates for creating different shapes, such as a tree, daisy, shell, star, fleur-de-lis, wreath, and snowflake. Choose a press that feels comfortable in your hands.

2 cups (10 oz/315 g)
all-purpose flour

½ teaspoon kosher salt

2 large egg yolks, at room
temperature

2 teaspoons heavy cream

1 teaspoon pure vanilla extract

1 teaspoon almond extract

1 cup (8 oz/250 g) unsalted butter,
at room temperature

⅔ cup (5 oz/155 g) sugar

**MAKES ABOUT
6 DOZEN COOKIES**

Preheat the oven to 375°F (190°C).

In a bowl, sift together the flour and salt. In a small bowl, whisk together the egg yolks, cream, and vanilla and almond extracts. Set aside.

In the bowl of a stand mixer fitted with the paddle attachment, beat together the butter and sugar on medium speed until light and fluffy, about 3 minutes. Reduce the speed to low, slowly add the egg yolk mixture, and beat until combined, about 1 minute. Stop the mixer and scrape down the sides of the bowl. Add the flour mixture and beat on low speed until combined, about 1 minute.

Turn the dough out onto a work surface and knead once or twice to bring it together.

Following the manufacturer's instructions, fill the barrel of a cookie press and form cookies onto an ungreased baking sheet, spacing them about 1 inch (2.5 cm) apart. Refrigerate for 10 minutes.

Bake until the cookies are light golden brown on the edges, 8–10 minutes. Transfer the cookies to a wire rack and let cool. Repeat with the remaining dough.

TIP *The key to using a cookie press with ease is the temperature of the dough. If the dough becomes too warm and soft, refrigerate for 5 minutes before pressing out more cookies. For a festive assortment, add food coloring to the dough or top the cookies with sprinkles after baking.*

Perfect Chocolate Chip Cookies

If using, choose a high-quality flaky sea salt, such as Jacobson or fleur de sel, for topping these iconic cookies. The salt deepens the chocolate flavor and tempers the sweetness. If you like, stir in 1 cup (4 oz/125 g) pecans or walnuts, toasted and coarsely chopped, with the chocolate chunks.

1¼ cups (6 1/2 oz/200 g) all-purpose flour

1 teaspoon baking soda

½ teaspoon salt

½ cup (4 oz/125 g) unsalted butter, at room temperature

½ cup (3½ oz/105 g) firmly packed light brown sugar

6 tablespoons (3 oz/90 g) granulated sugar

1 large egg

1 teaspoon vanilla extract

2½ cups (15 oz/470 g) semisweet chocolate chips

Flaky sea salt, for sprinkling (optional)

MAKES ABOUT 30 COOKIES

Preheat the oven to 350°F (180°C). Line 2 baking sheets with parchment paper.

In a bowl, sift together the flour, baking soda and salt. Set aside.

In a large bowl, using an electric mixer on medium speed, beat the butter, brown sugar and granulated sugar until smooth, about 2 minutes. Reduce the speed to low, add the egg and vanilla and mix until combined. Slowly add the flour mixture and mix just until incorporated. Stop the mixer and stir in the chocolate chips, distributing them evenly throughout the dough.

Drop the dough by rounded tablespoons onto the prepared baking sheet, spacing the cookies about 2 inches (5 cm) apart. Sprinkle the top of the cookies with sea salt, if using.

Bake the cookies, 1 sheet at a time, until the bottoms and edges are lightly browned and the tops feel firm when lightly touched, 10–13 minutes. Transfer the baking sheet to a wire rack and let the cookies cool on the sheet for 5 minutes, then transfer the cookies to the rack and let cook slightly before serving.

TIP *Cookie dough freezes well. Form into balls or rounded tablespoon shapes and freeze, wrapped in plastic wrap or placed in a zippered plastic bag. There's no need to thaw the dough; bake as many cookies as you want and increase the cooking time by 1 to 2 minutes.*

VARIATION

Salted-Caramel Chocolate Chip Cookies
Make the cookie dough as directed and scoop into 1½-tablespoon rounds. Cut 12 salted caramel candies in half. Press a caramel half into the center of each round and press the dough together to completely enclose the caramel. Roll into a ball and bake as directed, increasing the baking time to 10–12 minutes.

Chocolate Crinkle Cookies

With their textured tops and soft, chewy interiors, these cookies are crowd-pleasers. To boost the chocolate factor, roll the dough balls in equal parts confectioners' sugar and cocoa powder. Using room-temperature ingredients ensures that the dough comes together evenly and that the cookies all have the same texture.

1⅔ cups (8 ½ oz/265 g) all-purpose flour

½ cup (1½ oz/45 g) plus 1 tablespoon unsweetened cocoa powder or Dutch-process cocoa powder

1½ teaspoons baking powder

¼ teaspoon kosher salt

½ cup (4 oz/125 g) unsalted butter, at room temperature

1¼ cups (10 oz/315 g) granulated sugar

2 large eggs

½ teaspoon pure vanilla extract

½ cup (2 oz/60 g) confectioners' sugar

MAKES ABOUT 18 COOKIES

Preheat the oven to 350°F (180°C). Line a baking sheet with parchment paper.

In a bowl, sift together the flour, cocoa powder, baking powder, and salt. Set aside.

In the bowl of a stand mixer fitted with the paddle attachment, beat together the butter and granulated sugar on medium speed until light and fluffy, about 3 minutes. Reduce the speed to low and add the eggs one at a time, beating well after each addition. Add the vanilla and beat until combined, about 1 minute. Stop the mixer and scrape down the sides of the bowl. Add the flour mixture and beat on low speed until combined, about 1 minute.

Place the confectioners' sugar in a small bowl. Scoop up a rounded tablespoon of the dough and roll between your palms into a ball. Roll the ball in the confectioners' sugar and place on the prepared baking sheet. Repeat with the remaining dough, spacing the cookies about 2 inches (5 cm) apart. Flatten each ball slightly with the palm of your hand.

Bake until the cookies are crackled and puffed, 10–12 minutes. Transfer the baking sheet to a wire rack and let the cookies cool on the sheet for 3 minutes, then transfer the cookies to the rack and let cool slightly before serving.

Cowboy Cookies

Despite their name, these ingredient-packed cookies, which boast the texture and flavor of old-fashioned oatmeal cookies, appeal to more than denizens of the Wild West. If you have time, refrigerate the dough for 30 minutes to 1 hour before or after shaping to prevent the cookies from spreading too much in the hot oven.

1½ cups (7½ oz/235 g) all-purpose flour

2 teaspoons baking powder

1 teaspoon baking soda

1 teaspoon ground cinnamon

½ teaspoon kosher salt

¾ cup (6 oz/185 g) unsalted butter, at room temperature

¾ cup (6 oz/185 g) granulated sugar

¾ cup (6 oz/185 g) firmly packed dark brown sugar

2 large eggs

2 teaspoons pure vanilla extract

1 cup (6 oz/185 g) semisweet chocolate chips

2 cups (6 oz/185 g) rolled oats

¾ cup (3 oz/90 g) shredded dried unsweetened coconut

½ cup (2 oz/60 g) chopped walnuts

**MAKES ABOUT
2 DOZEN COOKIES**

Preheat the oven to 350°F (180°C). Line a baking sheet with parchment paper.

In a bowl, sift together the flour, baking powder, baking soda, cinnamon, and salt. Set aside.

In the bowl of a stand mixer fitted with the paddle attachment, beat together the butter, granulated sugar, and brown sugar on medium speed until light and fluffy, about 3 minutes. Reduce the speed to low, add the eggs one at a time, beating well after each addition. Add the vanilla and beat until combined, about 1 minute. Stop the mixer and scrape down the sides of the bowl. Add the flour mixture and beat on low speed until combined, about 1 minute. Stop the mixer and stir in the chocolate chips, oats, coconut, and walnuts.

Drop the dough by rounded tablespoons onto the prepared baking sheet, spacing the cookies about 3 inches (7.5 cm) apart.

Bake until the cookies are golden brown, 15–17 minutes. Transfer the cookies to a wire rack and let cool completely.

Mexican Wedding Cookies

In Mexico, where they are known as *polvorones*, these melt-in-your-mouth cookies are individually wrapped in tissue paper for serving at weddings and other celebrations. In the United States, similar cookies are called snowballs or Russian tea cakes. To vary the seasoning, replace the cinnamon with ground anise, or omit the spice altogether.

1¾ cups (9 oz/280 g) all-purpose flour

1 teaspoon ground cinnamon

1 cup (8 oz/250 g) unsalted butter, at room temperature

1½ cups (6 oz/185 g) confectioners' sugar

1 teaspoon pure vanilla extract

¼ teaspoon kosher salt

1 cup (5 oz/155 g) coarsely ground blanched almonds

**MAKES ABOUT
4 DOZEN COOKIES**

Preheat the oven to 350°F (180°C). Line a baking sheet with parchment paper.

In a bowl, sift together the flour and cinnamon. Set aside.

In the bowl of a stand mixer fitted with the paddle attachment, beat the butter on high speed until fluffy and pale yellow, about 3 minutes. Add ½ cup (2 oz/60 g) of the confectioners' sugar and beat until light and fluffy, about 2 minutes. Reduce the speed to low, add the vanilla and salt, and beat until combined, about 1 minute. Stop the mixer and scrape down the sides of the bowl. Add the flour mixture and beat on low speed until combined, about 1 minute. Stop the mixer and stir in the almonds.

Cover the bowl and refrigerate until the dough is chilled but not hard and is no longer sticky to the touch, about 15 minutes.

Shape the dough into 1-inch (2.5-cm) balls and place on the prepared baking sheet, spacing the cookies about 1 inch (2.5 cm) apart.

Bake until the cookies are just golden on the bottom, 10–12 minutes. Transfer the baking sheet to a wire rack and let the cookies cool on the sheet for 5 minutes.

Meanwhile, sift the remaining 1 cup (4 oz/125 g) confectioners' sugar into a shallow bowl. Roll the cookies one at a time in the confectioners' sugar, place on the rack, and let cool completely.

VARIATION

Honey & Rose Water Mexican Cookies

Preheat the oven and follow the directions, sifting the flour but omitting the cinnamon. Beat together the butter and ½ cup (6 oz/185 g) honey, omitting the ½ cup (2 oz/60 g) confectioners' sugar. Beat in 1 teaspoon rose water along with the vanilla and salt. Bake as directed.

Ginger-Molasses Cookies

Cookies that showcase ginger and molasses turn up everywhere, from New England to Scandinavia to the Czech Republic. This version, heady with ginger as well as cinnamon and allspice, pairs well with afternoon coffee or tea in the cool-weather months. For a bright citrus touch, mix in 2 teaspoons grated orange zest with the molasses.

2 cups (10 oz/315 g) all-purpose flour

1½ teaspoons baking soda

¼ teaspoon kosher salt

1½ teaspoons ground ginger

1 teaspoon ground cinnamon

½ teaspoon ground allspice

¾ cup (6 oz/185 g) unsalted butter, at room temperature

1 cup (7 oz/220 g) firmly packed light brown sugar

1 large egg

⅓ cup (3¾ oz/115 g) light molasses

½ cup (3½ oz/100 g) turbinado sugar

**MAKES ABOUT
3 DOZEN COOKIES**

Preheat the oven to 350°F (180°C). Line a baking sheet with parchment paper.

In a bowl, sift together the flour, baking soda, salt, ginger, cinnamon, and allspice. Set aside.

In the bowl of a stand mixer fitted with the paddle attachment, beat together the butter and brown sugar on medium speed until light and fluffy, about 3 minutes. Reduce the speed to low, add the egg and molasses, and beat until combined, about 1 minute. Stop the mixer and scrape down the sides of the bowl. Add the flour mixture and beat on low speed until combined, about 1 minute.

Drop the dough by rounded tablespoonfuls onto the prepared baking sheet, spacing the cookies about 2 inches (5 cm) apart. Sprinkle the cookies generously with the turbinado sugar.

Bake until the cookies are browned and firm to the touch, 10–12 minutes. Transfer the baking sheet to a wire rack and let the cookies cool on the sheet for 5 minutes, then transfer the cookies to the rack and let cool completely.

TIP *To add an extra kick of ginger, stir finely chopped candied ginger into the dough after beating in the flour mixture.*

Peanut Butter Cookies

Don't worry if all you have on hand is chunky peanut butter. This easy recipe will still work fine. To give these old-fashioned cookies a decorative finish, bake and cool them as directed, then use a spoonful of melted chocolate of your choice to fill in the grooves created by the fork tines.

1⅓ cups (7 oz/220 g) all-purpose flour

½ teaspoon baking powder

½ teaspoon baking soda

½ teaspoon kosher salt

½ cup (4 oz/125 g) unsalted butter, melted and cooled

½ cup (4 oz/125 g) granulated sugar

½ cup (3½ oz/105 g) firmly packed light brown sugar

1 cup (10 oz/315 g) creamy peanut butter

1 large egg

1 teaspoon pure vanilla extract

**MAKES ABOUT
20 COOKIES**

In a bowl, sift together the flour, baking powder, baking soda, and salt. Set aside.

In the bowl of a stand mixer fitted with the paddle attachment, beat together the butter, granulated sugar, brown sugar, peanut butter, egg, and vanilla on low speed until well combined, about 3 minutes. Stop the mixer and scrape down the sides of the bowl. Add the flour mixture and beat on low speed until combined, about 1 minute. Cover the bowl and refrigerate until the dough is firm, about 2 hours.

Preheat the oven to 350°F (180°C). Line a baking sheet with parchment paper.

Shape the dough into 1-inch (2.5-cm) balls and place on the prepared baking sheet, spacing the cookies about 2 inches (5 cm) apart. Using the tines of a fork dipped in flour, flatten each ball slightly and make a pattern of parallel indentations.

Bake until the cookies are golden brown, 10–12 minutes. Transfer the baking sheet to a wire rack and let the cookies cool on the sheet for 3 minutes, then transfer the cookies to the rack and let cool slightly before serving.

TIP *To measure the peanut butter, spray a measuring cup with nonstick cooking spray, then spoon the peanut butter into it. The peanut butter will slip out of the measuring cup easily, and the measuring cup will clean up effortlessly.*

Chuck's Madeleines

In the late 1950s, Chuck Williams began importing French bakeware for Williams Sonoma, and tinned madeleine pans were among the first items he stocked. This is his recipe for the little sponge cakes that are baked in scallop shell–shaped molds. Always butter your pan, even if it's labeled nonstick, as these delicate cookies can easily stick.

4 tablespoons (2 oz/60 g) unsalted butter, very soft, plus more for greasing

½ cup (2½ oz/75 g) all-purpose flour

½ teaspoon baking powder

1 large egg

¼ cup (2 oz/60 g) granulated sugar

2 teaspoons orange-flower water

Confectioners' sugar, for dusting

MAKES 1 DOZEN MADELEINES

Preheat the oven to 400°F (200°C). Generously butter a 12-mold madeleine pan.

In a bowl, sift together the flour and baking powder. Set aside.

In the bowl of a stand mixer fitted with the paddle attachment, beat together the egg, granulated sugar, and orange-flower water on medium speed until combined, about 30 seconds. Raise the speed to medium-high and beat until the mixture has quadrupled in bulk and is very thick, about 10 minutes. Stop the mixer and, using a rubber spatula, carefully fold in the flour mixture and then the butter.

Spoon the batter into the prepared molds, filling each about three-fourths full and leaving the batter mounded in the center of the wells.

Bake until the madeleines are lightly browned around the edges and on the bottom, 8–10 minutes. Immediately turn the madeleines out onto a wire rack. Using a fine-mesh sieve or a sifter, dust them with confectioners' sugar. Serve warm.

TIP *For an even more delicate texture, swap some or all of the all-purpose flour for cake flour. Make sure the butter is very soft so that it folds in easily.*

VARIATIONS

Almond Madeleines
Replace the orange-flower water with 2 teaspoons almond extract.

Lemon Madeleines
Replace the orange-flower water with 2 teaspooons grated lemon zest and 1 teaspoon fresh lemon juice.

Cherry & Hazelnut Chocolate-Dipped Biscotti

Also known as *cantucci*, these Italian biscuits are twice baked to achieve their signature crunchy texture. While coffee is a favorite accompaniment, dessert wines, notably Vin Santo, are another traditional pairing. Look for a wine with tasting notes of dark fruits or toasted nuts.

1¾ cups (7½ oz/210 g) plus 1 tablespoon all-purpose flour, plus more for dusting

½ teaspoon baking powder

¼ teaspoon kosher salt

½ teaspoon ground cinnamon

½ cup (4 oz/115 g) unsalted butter, at room temperature

¾ cup (5 oz/140 g) sugar

2 large eggs, at room temperature

2 teaspoons vanilla bean paste

1 cup (6 oz/170 g) dried tart cherries

¾ cup (3¾ oz/110 g) hazelnuts, toasted, skinned, and coarsely chopped

1 tablespoon Frangelico

1 teaspoon grated orange zest

1 cup (6 oz/170 g) semisweet chocolate chips

1 tablespoon canola oil

Flaky sea salt, for sprinkling

**MAKES ABOUT
3 DOZEN BISCOTTI**

Place 1 rack in the upper third and 1 rack in the lower third of the oven and preheat to 350°F (180°C). Line 2 baking sheets with parchment paper.

In a bowl, sift together the flour, baking powder, salt, and cinnamon. Set aside.

In the bowl of a stand mixer fitted with the paddle attachment, beat the butter on high speed until fluffy and pale yellow, about 2 minutes. Add the sugar and beat until combined, about 1 minute. Reduce the speed to low and add the eggs one at a time, beating well after each addition. Add the vanilla and beat until combined, about 1 minute. Stop the mixer and scrape down the sides of the bowl. Slowly add the flour mixture and beat on low speed until incorporated, about 2 minutes. Beat in the cherries, hazelnuts, Frangelico, and orange zest until evenly distributed. The dough should be very soft.

Turn the dough out onto a well-floured work surface and divide in half. Using well-floured hands, transfer half of the dough to 1 of the prepared baking sheets and shape into a log about 12 inches (30 cm) long and 1½ inches (4 cm) in diameter. Place on one side of the sheet. Repeat with the remaining dough, leaving at least 4 inches (10 cm) between the logs (they will spread a bit as they bake).

Bake until the edges of the logs are golden, 25–30 minutes. Transfer the baking sheet to a wire rack and let the logs cool for 10 minutes. Using a serrated knife, cut the logs, still on the sheet, on the diagonal into slices about ½ inch (12 mm) wide. Carefully turn the slices on their sides; when you run out of room on 1 baking sheet, start transferring slices to the other prepared baking sheet. Return both sheets to the oven, placing one sheet on the top rack and the other sheet on the lower rack.

Bake until the edges of the biscotti are golden, 10–12 minutes. Transfer the baking sheets to wire racks and let the biscotti cool completely on the sheets.

Meanwhile, line another baking sheet with parchment paper. Place the chocolate chips in a heatproof bowl set over but not touching barely simmering water in a saucepan and heat, stirring often, until melted and smooth. Whisk in the oil until smooth. Remove from the heat.

Dip one end of each biscotti into the melted chocolate, using a spoon to coat half of the biscotti with the chocolate. Carefully shake off the excess. Place on the prepared baking sheet and sprinkle with sea salt. Refrigerate until the chocolate is set, about 30 minutes.

Peppermint Crunch Cookies

Dutch-process cocoa powder gives these easy-to-make fudgy cookies a rich dark color and a deep chocolate taste. To infuse the white chocolate icing with peppermint flavor, add ½ teaspoon peppermint extract with the oil. Store these cookies between sheets of waxed or parchment paper to keep them looking their best.

FOR THE COOKIES

1¼ cups (6½ oz/200 g) all-purpose flour

¾ cup (6 oz/185 g) sugar

¾ cup (2¼ oz/65 g) Dutch-process cocoa powder

1 teaspoon baking soda

¼ teaspoon baking powder

¼ teaspoon kosher salt

¾ cup (6 oz/185 g) unsalted butter, at room temperature

1 large egg plus 1 large egg yolk

1 teaspoon peppermint extract

FOR THE ICING

2 cups (12 oz/375 g) white chocolate chips

2 tablespoons canola oil

15–20 peppermint candies, crushed (about ½ cup/85 g)

MAKES ABOUT 2 DOZEN COOKIES

Preheat the oven to 375°F (190°C). Line a baking sheet with parchment paper.

In the bowl of a stand mixer, using a handheld whisk, whisk together the flour, sugar, cocoa powder, baking soda, baking powder, and salt. Fit the mixer with the paddle attachment, add the butter, and beat on low speed until light and fluffy, about 3 minutes, then beat in the egg, egg yolk, and peppermint extract. Raise the speed to medium and beat until the dough comes together, about 2 minutes.

Drop the dough by rounded tablespoons onto the prepared baking sheet, spacing the cookies about 2 inches (5 cm) apart. Flatten each ball slightly with the palm of your hand.

Bake until the cookies are firm to the touch, 8–10 minutes. Transfer the baking sheet to a wire rack and let the cookies cool on the sheet for 5 minutes, then transfer the cookies to the rack and let cool completely.

Meanwhile, make the icing: Place the white chocolate chips in a heatproof bowl set over but not touching barely simmering water in a saucepan and heat, stirring occasionally, until the chocolate is melted. Remove from the heat and stir in the oil until smooth.

Line another baking sheet with parchment paper. Dip each cookie halfway into the melted white chocolate, then immediately sprinkle peppermint candies over the white chocolate. Place on the prepared baking sheet. If the white chocolate begins to harden, set the bowl over simmering water for up to 1 minute to remelt. Let the cookies set up for 15 minutes before serving.

TIP *For a different but still festive twist during the winter holidays, replace the peppermint candies with crushed peppermint bark.*

Gingerbread Cookies

You can add colorful decorations to these classic spice cookies using nonpareils, nonmetallic dragées, small candies, and cylindrical sprinkles. Pipe the icing onto the cookies as directed, then use tweezers to carefully arrange the decorations on the damp icing. A dusting of sanding sugar is also a great choice, as are dried currants and cranberries.

FOR THE COOKIES

5 cups (25 oz/780 g) all-purpose flour, plus more for dusting

1 teaspoon baking soda

½ teaspoon kosher salt

1 tablespoon ground ginger

1 teaspoon ground cinnamon

½ teaspoon ground cloves

1 cup (8 oz/250 g) unsalted butter, at room temperature

½ cup (4 oz/125 g) granulated sugar

½ cup (3½ oz/105 g) firmly packed light brown sugar

1 cup (11 oz/345 g) light molasses

1 large egg

FOR THE ICING

1 cup (4 oz/125 g) confectioners' sugar

2 tablespoons half-and-half

½ teaspoon fresh lemon juice

DEPENDING ON SIZE, MAKES 2–5 DOZEN COOKIES

In a large bowl, sift together the flour, baking soda, salt, ginger, cinnamon, and cloves. Set aside.

In the bowl of a stand mixer fitted with the paddle attachment, beat together the butter, granulated sugar, and brown sugar on medium speed until light and fluffy, about 3 minutes. Reduce the speed to low and gradually beat in the molasses. Add the egg and beat until combined, about 1 minute. Stop the mixer and scrape down the sides of the bowl. Add the flour mixture and beat on low speed until combined, about 1 minute.

Turn the dough out onto a work surface, divide into 4 equal pieces, and shape each into a disk. Wrap separately in plastic wrap and refrigerate for at least 1 hour or up to 2 days. Let the dough soften slightly at room temperature before continuing.

Preheat the oven to 400°F (200°C). Line a baking sheet with parchment paper.

On a well-floured work surface, roll out 1 dough disk ¼ inch (6 mm) thick. Using gingerbread cookie cutters 3–5 inches (7.5–13 cm) tall, cut out cookies. Transfer the cookies to the prepared baking sheet, spacing them about 1½ inches (4 cm) apart. Repeat with the remaining dough disks. Gather up the scraps of dough, reroll, and cut out more cookies. If the scraps have become sticky, refrigerate for 10 minutes before rerolling. For best results, do not roll the same piece of dough more than twice.

Bake until the cookies are lightly browned on the bottom, about 6 minutes. Transfer the baking sheet to a wire rack and let the cookies cool on the sheet for 5 minutes, then transfer the cookies to the rack and let cool completely.

Meanwhile, make the icing: In a bowl, whisk together the confectioners' sugar, half-and-half, and lemon juice until completely smooth. Transfer to a piping bag fitted with a fine tip and decorate the cookies as desired.

TIP *If the icing is too thin, add more confectioners' sugar. If it is too thick, stir in more half-and-half until it reaches the desired consistency.*

Candy Cane Cookies

These whimsical cookies are easy to shape if you refrigerate the dough overnight as directed. If you would like less peppermint flavor, substitute ½ teaspoon pure vanilla extract for half of the peppermint extract. For a decorative finish, stir together about 1½ tablespoons each finely crushed peppermint candy and sugar and sprinkle over the just-baked cookies.

1 recipe Sugar Cookies (page 210)

1 teaspoon peppermint extract

1 teaspoon red food coloring, plus more as needed

All-purpose flour, for dusting

**MAKES ABOUT
2 DOZEN COOKIES**

Make the cookie dough. Divide the dough into 2 equal pieces. Place 1 piece in the bowl of a stand mixer fitted with the paddle attachment and mix in the peppermint extract and red food coloring until completely combined. Shape each piece into a disk, wrap separately in plastic wrap, and refrigerate overnight. Let the dough soften slightly at room temperature before continuing.

Preheat the oven to 350°F (180°C). Line a baking sheet with parchment paper.

On a lightly floured work surface, roll out each dough disk ¼ inch (6 mm) thick. Cut into strips 6 inches (15 cm) long and ¾ inch (2 cm) wide. Taking 1 red strip and 1 plain strip, pinch the ends together and gently twist the strips around each other. Pinch the other end to secure and bend one end into a hook to form a candy cane shape. Transfer to the prepared baking sheet. Repeat with the remaining dough, spacing the cookies about 1½ inches (4 cm) apart.

Bake until the cookies are golden on the edges, about 8 minutes. Transfer the cookies to a wire rack and let cool completely.

TIP *You can also roll each disk of dough into long, skinny ropes about ½ inch (12 mm) thick and cut into 6-inch (15-cm) lengths before twisting.*

Minty Chocolate Meringues

These pretty cookies use a Swiss meringue, which calls for heating the egg whites and sugar together before beating. It yields a denser, smoother, and more stable meringue than a French meringue, which incorporates the sugar as the whites are beaten. Don't adjust the amount of sugar, as the structure of any meringue depends on the correct ratio of egg whites to sugar.

7 large egg whites

2 cups (1 lb/500 g) sugar

1 teaspoon peppermint extract

5 tablespoons (1 oz/30 g) Dutch-process cocoa powder, sifted

¼ lb (125 g) bittersweet chocolate, finely chopped

¼ lb (125 g) cacao nibs

**MAKES ABOUT
4 DOZEN COOKIES**

Preheat the oven to 350°F (180°C). Line a baking sheet with parchment paper.

In a heatproof bowl, whisk together the egg whites and sugar until combined. Set the bowl over but not touching barely simmering water in a saucepan and whisk constantly until the sugar is completely dissolved, about 3 minutes. Remove the bowl from the heat and whisk in the peppermint extract.

In the bowl of a stand mixer fitted with the whisk attachment, beat the egg white mixture on high speed until stiff, glossy peaks form, about 8 minutes. Stop the mixer and add the cocoa powder, chocolate, and cacao nibs. Gently fold into the meringue until just combined.

Drop the meringue by heaping tablespoonfuls onto the prepared baking sheet, spacing the cookies about 1 inch (2.5 cm) apart.

Bake until the cookies are dry to the touch and begin to crack, 8–10 minutes. Transfer the baking sheet to a wire rack and let the cookies cool on the sheet for 5 minutes, then transfer the cookies to the rack and let cool completely.

TIP *For showstopping Christmas cookies, let the meringues cool completely, then dip in melted chocolate and sprinkle with crushed candy canes. You can also transfer the meringue to a piping bag fitted with a large decorating tip and pipe out intricately shaped cookies.*

Chocolate-Dipped Meringues

Piping these cookies with a decorating tip will add an effortlessly elegant touch. You can reserve the egg yolks for another use, such as omelets, French toast, or Lemon Curd (page 222).

4 large egg whites

1 tablespoon cornstarch

1 cup (7 oz/200 g) sugar

1 teaspoon pure vanilla extract

Pinch of kosher salt

2 teaspoons Dutch-process cocoa powder, sifted

¼ lb (115 g) bittersweet chocolate, cut into pieces

1 tablespoon vegetable oil

**MAKES ABOUT
3 DOZEN COOKIES**

Place 1 rack in the upper third and 1 rack in the lower third of the oven and preheat to 200°F (95°C). Line 2 baking sheets with parchment paper.

In the bowl of a stand mixer fitted with the whisk attachment, beat the egg whites on medium speed until combined, about 1 minute. Sprinkle the cornstarch over the whites and beat until foamy, about 3 minutes. Raise the speed to high, very gradually add the sugar, and beat until stiff, shiny peaks form, about 8–10 minutes. Quickly beat in the vanilla.

Transfer half of the meringue to a pastry bag fitted with a star tip. Set aside.

Using a rubber spatula, gently fold the salt and cocoa powder into the remaining meringue until just combined. Transfer the chocolate meringue to another pastry bag fitted with a star tip. Using the chocolate meringue, pipe stars 1 inch (2.5 cm) wide on 1 of the prepared baking sheets, spacing them about ½ inch (12 mm) apart. Repeat with the plain meringue on the other baking sheet.

Bake, rotating the baking sheets between the racks halfway through baking, until the meringues are dry, crisp, and firm, 1½–2 hours. Turn off the oven, prop the door open, and let the meringues cool in the oven for about 1 hour. Transfer the meringues, still on the parchment, to wire racks and let cool completely.

Line the baking sheets with fresh sheets of parchment paper. Place the chocolate in a heatproof bowl set over but not touching barely simmering water in a saucepan and heat, stirring often, until melted and smooth. Whisk in the oil until smooth. Remove from the heat.

Dip the bottom of each meringue into the melted chocolate, letting the excess drip off. Place, chocolate side down, on the prepared baking sheet. Freeze until the chocolate is set, about 3 minutes.

Chocolate–Coconut Macaroons

An ideal gluten-free treat, these macaroons are delicious and decadent for any occasion. For a more intense coconut flavor, spread the shredded coconut on a baking sheet and toast in the preheated oven just until it begins to color, about 6 minutes, and let cool before using.

3½ cups (14 oz/440 g) shredded dried sweetened coconut

¾ cup (6 oz/185 g) sugar

5 large egg whites, lightly beaten

1½ teaspoons pure vanilla extract

¼ teaspoon almond extract

¾ lb (375 g) bittersweet or semisweet chocolate, finely chopped

MAKES ABOUT 18 MACAROONS

Line a baking sheet with parchment paper. In a bowl, combine the coconut, sugar, egg whites, and vanilla and almond extracts and stir well. Spread on the prepared baking sheet and refrigerate until cold, about 30 minutes.

Preheat the oven to 300°F (150°C). Line another baking sheet with parchment paper.

Scoop up the coconut mixture by heaping tablespoonfuls and pack into small, rounded domes. Place on the prepared baking sheet.

Bake until the macaroons are golden, about 30 minutes. Transfer the macaroons to a wire rack and let cool completely. Line the baking sheet with a fresh sheet of parchment paper.

Place the chocolate in a heatproof bowl set over but not touching barely simmering water in a saucepan and heat, stirring often, until melted and smooth. Remove the bowl from over the water. Dip the bottom of each macaroon in the melted chocolate to a depth of about ¼ inch (6 mm). Place, chocolate side down, on the prepared baking sheet. Refrigerate until the chocolate is firm, about 1 hour.

TIP *These macaroons are great make-ahead cookies. Refrigerate them in an airtight container for up to 3 days. Let stand at room temperature for about 1 hour before serving.*

Alfajores with Buttered Rum & Vanilla Bean Filling

Alfajores are made in many countries with countless variations. Traditionally filled with dulce de leche, the cookies can also be filled with jams or other fillings. This yummy variation of the classic version features a rum-flavored filling—perfect for rum lovers. Save your fresh vanilla pod for future baking recipes, or make vanilla sugar by placing it in a jar of granulated sugar.

FOR THE DOUGH

2 cups (10 oz/315 g) all-purpose flour, plus more for dusting

2 tablespoons cornstarch

½ teaspoon kosher salt

¾ cup (6 oz/185 g) cold unsalted butter, cut into cubes

½ cup (2 oz/60 g) confectioners' sugar

2 teaspoons pure vanilla extract

2 large egg yolks

FOR THE FILLING

2 cups (14 oz/440 g) firmly packed light brown sugar

1 cup (250 ml) heavy cream

4 tablespoons (2 oz/60 g) unsalted butter

½ teaspoon kosher salt

3 tablespoons aged rum

1 vanilla bean, split, with seeds scraped and reserved

MAKES ABOUT 1 DOZEN SANDWICH COOKIES

To make the filling, in a saucepan over medium heat, combine the brown sugar, cream, butter, and salt. Cook, stirring frequently, until the mixture begins to simmer, about 3 minutes. Reduce the heat to medium-low and cook, stirring frequently, until thickened, about 15 minutes. Remove from the heat, stir in the rum and vanilla bean seeds, and transfer to a bowl. Let cool to room temperature, then cover and refrigerate until firm, about 1 hour.

Preheat the oven to 325°F (165°C). Line a baking sheet with parchment paper.

In a food processor, combine the flour, cornstarch, and salt and pulse until blended. Add the butter and pulse until the texture resembles fine crumbs. Add the confectioners' sugar, vanilla, and egg yolks and process until the dough comes together in a single mass.

Turn the dough out onto a well-floured surface and roll out ¼ inch (6 mm) thick. Using a 2-inch (5-cm) round cutter, cut out cookies. Transfer the cookies to the prepared baking sheet, spacing them about 1½ inches (4 cm) apart. Gather up the scraps of dough, reroll, and cut out more cookies, refrigerating the dough for 15 minutes if it gets too warm.

Bake until the cookies are lightly golden brown on the edges, 13–15 minutes. Transfer the baking sheet to a wire rack and let cool completely.

Spread about 1 tablespoon of the buttered rum filling on the flat side of half of the cookies. Top with the remaining cookies, flat side down, and gently press together, filling the cookies with the filling.

TIP *To scrape out the seeds of a vanilla bean, use a small knife to cut the bean in half lengthwise. Use the back of the knife to scrape out the seeds from the inside of the pod. If you don't have a vanilla bean, substitute 1 tablespoon of pure vanilla extract instead.*

Rugelach with Apricot & Pistachio Filling

You can't rush the preparation of these traditional Jewish treats, but you can make them ahead: Freeze the shaped cookies on a baking sheet, transfer to an airtight container, and freeze for up to 1 month. Bake them straight from the freezer, adding a few minutes to the baking time.

FOR THE DOUGH

1 cup (5 oz/155 g) plus
2 tablespoons all-purpose flour, plus more for dusting

¼ teaspoon kosher salt

½ cup (4 oz/125 g) unsalted butter, cut into small pieces, at room temperature

¼ lb (125 g) cream cheese, cut into small pieces, at room temperature

2 tablespoons granulated sugar

FOR THE FILLING

¾ cup (4½ oz/140 g) dried apricots, halved

2 tablespoons granulated sugar

¼ teaspoon ground cinnamon

¼ cup (1 oz/30 g) finely chopped unsalted pistachios, plus more for sprinkling

1 large egg beaten with 1 teaspoon water

Turbinado sugar, for sprinkling

MAKES 2 DOZEN COOKIES

To make the dough, in a bowl, sift together the flour and salt. Set aside.

In the bowl of a stand mixer fitted with the paddle attachment, beat together the butter and cream cheese on medium speed until smooth and combined, about 3 minutes. Add the granulated sugar and beat until combined, about 2 minutes. Stop the mixer and scrape down the sides of the bowl. Add the flour mixture and beat on low speed until combined, about 1 minute. Turn the dough out onto a floured work surface, divide into 4 equal pieces, and shape each into a disk. Wrap separately in plastic and refrigerate for at least 2 hours or up to 6 hours.

Meanwhile, make the filling: In a saucepan over low heat, combine the apricots and ½ cup (125 ml) water. Cover and cook, stirring occasionally, until the fruit absorbs the water, 10–15 minutes. Let cool slightly, then transfer to a food processor and process to a smooth purée. Transfer to a bowl and stir in the granulated sugar, cinnamon, and pistachios. Set aside.

Preheat the oven to 350°F (180°C). Line a baking sheet with parchment paper.

On a lightly floured work surface, roll out 1 dough disk into a 7-inch (18-cm) circle about ¼ inch (6 mm) thick. Spread ¼ of the filling evenly over the top. Using a large knife, cut the dough into 6 wedges. Starting at the outside edge, gently roll up each wedge toward the point. (If needed, use a thin metal spatula to loosen the wedges from the work surface.) If the dough becomes too soft to roll, refrigerate for about 5 minutes to firm up. Transfer the rolled cookies to the prepared baking sheet, spacing them about 2 inches (5 cm) apart. Repeat with the remaining dough and filling, flouring the work surface as needed. Lightly brush the cookies with the egg mixture, then sprinkle with a pinch each of chopped pistachios and turbinado sugar.

Bake until the cookies are golden brown, 18–20 minutes. Transfer the baking sheet to a wire rack and let the cookies cool on the sheet for 5 minutes, then transfer the cookies to the rack and let cool completely.

TIP *Because this is a sticky dough, you may find it easier to place it between two sheets of waxed paper and then roll it out.*

Homemade Oreos

Here, Oreos, the best-selling cookie in the United States for more than a century, are re-created in the home kitchen. If you don't have a piping bag, fill a plastic bag half full with the filling. Twist the top closed and snip off about ¼ inch (6 mm) from a bottom corner.

FOR THE COOKIES

1¼ cups (6½ oz/200 g) all-purpose flour, plus more for dusting

¾ cup (6 oz/185 g) granulated sugar

¾ cup (2¼ oz/65 g) unsweetened Dutch-process cocoa powder

1 teaspoon baking soda

¼ teaspoon baking powder

¼ teaspoon kosher salt

¾ cup (6 oz/185 g) unsalted butter, at room temperature

1 large egg plus 1 large egg yolk

FOR THE FILLING

½ cup (4 oz/125 g) unsalted butter, at room temperature

1½ cups (6 oz/185 g) confectioners' sugar

1 tablespoon whole milk

1 teaspoon pure vanilla extract

MAKES ABOUT 1 DOZEN SANDWICH COOKIES

To make the cookies, preheat the oven to 375°F (190°C). Line a baking sheet with parchment paper.

In the bowl of a stand mixer fitted with the whisk attachment, whisk together the flour, granulated sugar, cocoa powder, baking soda, baking powder, and salt. Fit the mixer with the paddle attachment, add the butter, and beat on low speed until incorporated, about 2 minutes, then beat in the egg and egg yolk. Raise the speed to medium and beat until the dough comes together, about 2 minutes.

Turn the dough out onto a well-floured surface and roll out ¼ inch (6 mm) thick. Using a 2-inch (5-cm) round cutter, cut out cookies. Transfer the cookies to the prepared baking sheet, spacing them about 2 inches (5 cm) apart. Gather up the scraps of dough, reroll, and cut out more cookies, refrigerating the dough for 15 minutes if it gets too warm.

Bake until the cookies are firm to the touch, 8–10 minutes. Transfer the baking sheet to a wire rack and let the cookies cool on the sheet for 5 minutes, then transfer the cookies to the rack and let cool completely.

Meanwhile, make the filling: In the clean bowl of the stand mixer fitted with the clean paddle attachment, beat together the butter, confectioners' sugar, milk, and vanilla on medium-high speed until smooth and well combined, about 3 minutes. Transfer to a pastry bag fitted with a ½-inch (12-mm) tip.

Pipe a layer of the filling (about 2 teaspoons) on the flat side of half of the cookies. Top with the remaining cookies, flat side down, and gently press together.

TIP *To give your Oreos a mint flavor, add 1 teaspoon peppermint extract with the egg and egg yolk.*

Linzer Cookies

These crumbly, buttery, jam-packed cookies are named for the Austrian city of Linz. They can be sandwiched with nearly any jam, including raspberry, apricot, blackberry, strawberry, or black currant. For a pretty presentation, use a small decorative cutter—a star, heart, or diamond, for example—to cut the window in each top cookie.

1 cup (5 oz/155 g) hazelnuts, toasted and skinned, or slivered almonds, toasted

½ cup (4 oz/125 g) unsalted butter, at room temperature

½ cup (4 oz/125 g) granulated sugar

1 large egg yolk

1 teaspoon finely grated orange or lemon zest

¾ teaspoon pure vanilla extract

¼ teaspoon almond extract

1 cup (5 oz/155 g) all-purpose flour

½ teaspoon ground cinnamon

¼ teaspoon kosher salt

About ¼ cup (2½ oz/75 g) seedless raspberry jam

Confectioners' sugar, for dusting

**MAKES ABOUT 18
SANDWICH COOKIES**

In a food processor, finely grind the hazelnuts using short pulses. Set aside. In a large bowl, using an electric mixer on high speed, cream the butter until fluffy and pale yellow. Add the granulated sugar and continue beating until combined. Add the egg yolk, orange zest, vanilla, and almond extract and beat on low speed until well blended.

Sift the flour, cinnamon, and salt together into another bowl. Add the ground hazelnuts and stir to blend. Add the flour-nut mixture to the butter mixture and mix on low speed or stir with a wooden spoon until blended. The dough should be soft. Turn the dough out, divide into 4 equal pieces, and wrap each in plastic wrap. Refrigerate until chilled, about 1 hour.

Preheat the oven to 350°F (180°C). Line 2 baking sheets with parchment paper. Remove 1 piece of the dough at a time from the refrigerator, place between 2 sheets of waxed paper, and roll out ¼ inch (6 mm) thick. Using a cookie cutter about 2½ inches (6 cm) in diameter, cut out the cookies. Repeat to roll out the remaining dough portions, then reroll the dough scraps to make 36 cookies total. If the dough becomes sticky, wrap it in plastic wrap and chill in the freezer for about 10 minutes before rolling out. Cut a hole in the center of 18 of the cookies using a 1¼-inch (3-cm) cutter.

Using a thin spatula, carefully transfer the cookies to the prepared baking sheets. Bake until firm to the touch, about 12 minutes. Transfer the baking sheets to wire racks. Loosen the cookies from the baking sheets with the spatula, but let the cookies cool on the sheets.

To assemble, spread the solid cookies with about 1 teaspoon of the raspberry jam, leaving a ¼-inch (6-mm) border. Top the solid cookies with the cutout cookies, pressing them together gently. Using a fine-mesh sieve, dust the cookies with confectioners' sugar.

TIP *Metal cookie cutters give the cutout dough shapes cleaner, more defined edges than plastic cookie cutters.*

Lemon Cream Sandwich Cookies

For a fancier finish, skip the dusting of confectioners' sugar. Instead, melt ¾ cup (4½ oz/140 g) white chocolate chips in a bowl over but not touching barely simmering water in a saucepan, stirring until smooth. Dip half of each cookie in the chocolate and then in a bowl of finely chopped toasted nuts of choice. Place on parchment or waxed paper until the chocolate sets.

FOR THE COOKIES

2 cups (10 oz/315 g) all-purpose flour, plus more as needed

½ teaspoon baking powder

¼ teaspoon kosher salt

¾ cup (6 oz/185 g) unsalted butter, at room temperature

½ cup (4 oz/125 g) granulated sugar

3 large egg yolks

1 teaspoon pure vanilla extract

2 teaspoons grated lemon zest

2 tablespoons fresh lemon juice

FOR THE FILLING

¼ lb (125 g) cream cheese, at room temperature

4 tablespoons (2 oz/60 g) unsalted butter, at room temperature

1½ teaspoons grated lemon zest

3 tablespoons fresh lemon juice

½ cup (2 oz/60 g) confectioners' sugar, plus more for dusting

¼ teaspoon kosher salt

MAKES ABOUT 2 DOZEN SANDWICH COOKIES

To make the cookies, in a bowl, sift together the flour, baking powder, and salt. Set aside.

In the bowl of a stand mixer fitted with the paddle attachment, beat together the butter and granulated sugar on medium speed until light and fluffy, about 3 minutes. Reduce the speed to low, add the egg yolks, vanilla, and lemon zest and juice and beat until combined, about 1 minute. Stop the mixer and scrape down the sides of the bowl. Add the flour mixture and beat on low speed until combined, about 1 minute. If the dough is still sticky, beat in more flour, 1–2 tablespoons at a time, until it is no longer sticky. Turn the dough out onto a work surface, divide into 2 equal pieces, and shape each into a disk. Wrap separately in plastic wrap and refrigerate for at least 30 minutes or up to overnight. Let the dough soften slightly at room temperature before continuing.

Preheat the oven to 350°F (180°C). Line a baking sheet with parchment paper.

On a lightly floured work surface, roll out 1 dough disk ⅛ inch (3 mm) thick. Using a 2-inch (5-cm) round cutter, cut out cookies. Transfer the cookies to the prepared baking sheet, spacing them about 2 inches (5 cm) apart. Repeat with the remaining dough disk.

Bake until the cookies are firm to the touch and the edges are golden brown, 10–11 minutes. Transfer to a wire rack and let cool completely.

Meanwhile, make the filling: In the clean bowl of the stand mixer fitted with a clean paddle attachment, beat together the cream cheese, butter, lemon zest and juice, confectioners' sugar, and salt on high speed until fluffy, about 3 minutes.

Spread about 1 tablespoon of the filling on the flat side of half of the cookies. Top with the remaining cookies, flat side down, and gently press together. Just before serving, dust the cookies with confectioners' sugar.

Millionaire Shortbread

The crisp layers alone make these bars an instant showstopper, but their chocolaty, salty-sweet flavor profile takes them over the top. If you opt for the sea salt garnish, use a high-quality variety such as Jacobson or fleur de sel for best results.

FOR THE CRUST

½ cup (4 oz/115 g) cold unsalted butter, cut into ½-inch (12-mm) pieces, plus more for greasing

1 cup (4 oz/115 g) all-purpose flour

¼ cup (2 oz/60 g) firmly packed dark brown sugar

2½ teaspoons cornstarch

½ teaspoon kosher salt

2 tablespoons cold water

1 large egg yolk

FOR THE CARAMEL

1 can (14 fl oz/425 ml) sweetened condensed milk

½ cup (3½ oz/100 g) plus 2 tablespoons firmly packed dark brown sugar

7 tablespoons (3½ oz/100 g) unsalted butter, cut into 1-inch (2.5-cm) pieces

2 tablespoons light corn syrup

1½ teaspoons pure vanilla extract

½ teaspoon kosher salt

1½ cups (8 oz/ 225 g) semisweet chocolate chips

¼ cup (60 ml) heavy cream

Flaky sea salt, for sprinkling (optional)

MAKES ABOUT 18 BARS

To make the crust, preheat the oven to 350°F (180°C). Line a 9-inch (23-cm) square baking dish with aluminum foil, pushing the foil into the corners and letting it overhang on all sides by about 2 inches (5 cm). Grease the foil.

In a food processor, combine the flour, brown sugar, cornstarch, and salt and pulse until blended. Add the butter and pulse until the mixture resembles coarse cornmeal. Add the water and egg yolk and process until moist clumps form and the dough just begins to come together. Transfer the dough to the prepared dish and press evenly into the bottom of the dish. Pierce the dough all over with a fork.

Bake until the crust is golden brown, about 20 minutes. Transfer the pan to a wire rack and let the crust cool while you make the caramel.

To make the caramel, in a saucepan over medium heat, whisk together the sweetened condensed milk and brown sugar. Add the butter, corn syrup, vanilla, and salt and bring to a gentle boil, whisking constantly, until the mixture has darkened slightly, is thickened, and registers 220°F (104°C) on a candy thermometer, 7–10 minutes. If the mixture starts to scorch, reduce the heat. Pour the caramel over the warm crust and let cool until the caramel is set, about 20 minutes.

In a microwave-safe bowl, combine the chocolate chips and cream and microwave in 30-second increments, stirring in between, until the chocolate is almost completely melted, then stir until no lumps remain. Pour the chocolate over the set caramel and spread evenly. Sprinkle the warm chocolate with sea salt (if using).

Refrigerate the bars until firm, at least 2 hours or up to overnight. Use the foil to lift the dessert from the dish and transfer to a cutting board. Cut into 2-inch (5-cm) squares and serve.

TIP *These bars can be stored in an airtight container in the refrigerator for up to 3 days.*

Shortbread Cookies

Scotland is the birthplace of shortbread, but nowadays, everybody everywhere is hooked on this buttery, crumbly cookie. For best results, buy the finest butter you can and make sure it is at room temperature before you begin beating to safeguard against dense, tough cookies.

2 cups (10 oz/315 g) all-purpose flour, plus more for dusting

½ teaspoon kosher salt

1 cup (8 oz/250 g) unsalted butter, at room temperature

½ cup (4 oz/125 g) sugar

2 teaspoons pure vanilla extract

**MAKES ABOUT
3 DOZEN COOKIES**

In a bowl, sift together the flour and salt. Set aside.

In the bowl of a stand mixer fitted with the paddle attachment, beat together the butter and sugar on medium speed until light and fluffy, about 3 minutes. Reduce the speed to low, add the vanilla, and beat until combined, about 1 minute. Stop the mixer and scrape down the sides of the bowl. Add the flour mixture and beat on low speed until combined, about 1 minute.

Turn the dough out onto a work surface and shape into a disk. Wrap in plastic wrap and refrigerate for 30 minutes.

Preheat the oven to 350°F (180°C). Line a baking sheet with parchment paper.

On a well-floured work surface, roll out the dough ¼ inch (6 mm) thick. Using a large knife, cut into 2-inch (5-cm) squares, then cut each square in half to create triangles. Transfer the cookies to the prepared baking sheet, spacing them about 1½ inches (4 cm) apart. Bake until the cookies are just golden brown on the edges, 12–14 minutes. Transfer the cookies to a wire rack and let cool completely.

TIP *Shortbread is endlessly customizable. We love the matcha variation, or you can blend citrus zest, finely ground Earl Grey tea, or dried lavender into the dough.*

VARIATION

Matcha Shortbread Cookies
Make the cookie dough as directed, whisking ¼ cup (1 oz/32 g) matcha powder into the flour and salt mixture. Beat the flour mixture into the butter mixture, then beat in 2 teaspoons heavy cream until combined. Refrigerate the dough and bake as directed.

Brown Butter–Crispy Rice Treats

The brown butter in this classic childhood staple lends an appealing nuttiness, making the revamped salty-sweet treat a go-to for adults and kids alike. To more easily cut the bars, coat your knife with nonstick cooking spray.

Nonstick cooking spray

5 tablespoons (2½ oz/70 g) unsalted butter, cut into pieces

1 lb (450 g) marshmallows

½ teaspoon pure vanilla extract

6 cups (6 oz/170 g) crisp rice cereal

Flaky sea salt, for sprinkling

MAKES 25 BARS

Lightly coat an 8-inch (20-cm) square baking dish with nonstick cooking spray. Line with parchment paper and lightly coat the parchment.

In a large saucepan over medium heat, melt the butter, swirling the pan occasionally, until starting to foam, about 3 minutes. Continue cooking until the butter turns a deep golden color and smells nutty, 5–7 minutes longer. Watch the butter carefully at the end to prevent it from burning. Add the marshmallows and cook, stirring occasionally, until melted, about 2 minutes. Remove from the heat and stir in the vanilla. Add the crisp rice cereal and stir until well coated.

Transfer the mixture to the prepared baking dish and spread evenly, pressing down to compact slightly. Sprinkle with sea salt. Let stand until set, about 15 minutes, then cut into 1½-inch (4-cm) squares.

TIP *Spray a little nonstick cooking spray onto your knife to make cutting the treats easier.*

Pumpkin Whoopie Pies

Serve these delectable treats, full of the flavors of fall, with a steaming mug of hot apple cider or herbal tea, garnished with a cinnamon stick.

1½ cups (7½ oz/235 g) all-purpose flour

1 teaspoon kosher salt

½ teaspoon baking powder

½ teaspoon baking soda

2 tablespoons ground cinnamon

2 teaspoons ground ginger

1 teaspoon ground cloves

1 can (15 oz) pumpkin purée

½ cup (125 ml) vegetable oil

1 large egg

1 teaspoon vanilla extract

1⅓ cups (10¼ oz/275 g) firmly packed dark brown sugar

Cream Cheese Frosting (page 225)

MAKES 12 WHOOPIE PIES

Preheat the oven to 350°F (180°C). Line 2 baking sheets with parchment paper.

In a medium bowl, whisk together the flour, salt, baking powder, baking soda, cinnamon, ginger, and cloves. Set aside.

In a large bowl, whisk together the pumpkin purée, oil, egg, vanilla, and brown sugar. Sprinkle the flour mixture over the pumpkin mixture and whisk just until the flour mixture disappears. Place a large disposable pastry bag in a container or drinking glass. Pour the batter into the bag and twist the top to close it. Cut off the tip of the bag to make a ½-inch (12 mm) opening and pipe out 24 rounds, each 2 inches (2 cm) wide, onto the prepared baking sheets, spacing the rounds at least 1 inch (2.5 cm) apart.

Bake until the cookies are shiny on top and dark golden brown, about 15 minutes. Have an adult help you transfer the cookies to a wire rack and let cool completely.

Place another large disposable pastry bag in a container or drinking glass. Transfer the cream cheese frosting into the bag and twist the top to close it. Cut off the tip of the bag to make a ¼-inch (6 mm) opening and pipe about 2 tablespoons frosting onto the flat side of half of the cooled cookies. Top each with a second cookie, flat side down, and press together to spread the frosting to the edge. Store in an airtight container in the refrigerator for up to 2 days.

Chocolate-Pecan Pie Bars

With a chocolate crust and plenty of chopped bittersweet chocolate, these bars are the perfect treat for any chocolate-and-pecan lover. They are also excellent for taking along on a picnic or to a potluck dinner.

1 recipe Chocolate Pie Dough (page 214)

3 large eggs

¾ cup (3¾ oz/115 g) light corn syrup

½ cup (3½ oz/105 g) firmly packed dark brown sugar

½ teaspoon kosher salt

4 tablespoons (2 oz/60 g) unsalted butter, melted and cooled

1 teaspoon pure vanilla extract

2 tablespoons heavy cream

2½ cups (10 oz/315 g) pecans, toasted and chopped

½ lb (250 g) bittersweet chocolate, chopped

Sea salt, for sprinkling

SERVES 10-12

Make the pie dough. On a lightly floured work surface, roll out the dough into an 11-by-15-inch (28-by-38-cm) rectangle. Roll the dough around the rolling pin and unroll it into a 9-by-13-inch (23-by-33-cm) baking dish. Gently press the dough into the bottom and sides of the dish. Trim the overhang to ½ inch (12 mm), fold the edge under itself, and decoratively flute or crimp. Freeze for 30 minutes.

Meanwhile, preheat the oven to 350°F (180°C).

Line the crust with aluminum foil and fill with pie weights. Bake until lightly browned, about 20 minutes. Remove the foil and pie weights and set on a wire rack to cool completely. Keep the oven set.

In a large bowl, stir together the eggs, corn syrup, brown sugar, kosher salt, melted butter, vanilla, and cream until smooth and blended. Stir in the pecans and chocolate. Pour the filling into the crust.

Bake until the center is slightly puffed and firm to the touch, 30–40 minutes, covering the edges with aluminum foil if they brown too quickly. Let cool on a wire rack until just slightly warm, about 45 minutes, before serving. Sprinkle with sea salt and cut into bars.

TIP *Instead of making the bars in a rectangular baking dish, feel free to use a 9-inch (23-cm) pie dish.*

Lemon Bars

These sweet-tart bars are guaranteed to disappear quickly at any gathering. Take the time to refrigerate the crust before baking to ensure it will crisp and brown in the oven. For a hint of lemon flavor in the crust, add 1 teaspoon grated lemon zest with the flour and sugar.

FOR THE CRUST

1¼ cups (6½ oz/200 g) all-purpose flour

½ cup (2 oz/60 g) confectioners' sugar

¼ cup (1 oz/30 g) cornstarch

½ teaspoon kosher salt

½ cup (4 oz/125 g) plus 3 tablespoons cold unsalted butter, cut into ½-inch (12-mm) pieces

1 tablespoon cold water

FOR THE FILLING

3 large eggs plus 3 large egg yolks

1 cup (8 oz/250 g) granulated sugar

3 tablespoons all-purpose flour

½ teaspoon kosher salt

3 teaspoons grated lemon zest

¾ cup (180 ml) fresh lemon juice

⅓ cup (80 ml) whole milk

Confectioners' sugar, for dusting

MAKES 16 BARS

To make the crust, preheat the oven to 350°F (180°C). Lightly grease an 8-inch (20-cm) square baking dish. Line with parchment paper, letting the paper overhang on two opposite sides by 2 inches (5 cm).

In a food processor, combine the flour, confectioners' sugar, cornstarch, and salt and pulse until blended. Add the butter and pulse until the mixture is coarse and pale yellow, 8–10 pulses. Add the cold water and pulse until just combined, 2–4 pulses.

Sprinkle the mixture into the prepared dish and press firmly into an even layer ¼–½ inch (6–12 mm) thick over the bottom of the dish and about ½ inch (12 mm) up the sides. Refrigerate for 20 minutes.

Bake until the crust is golden brown, 25–30 minutes. Reduce the oven temperature to 325°F (165°C).

To make the filling, in a bowl, whisk together the eggs, egg yolks, granulated sugar, flour, salt, lemon zest and juice, and milk until combined. Pour the filling on top of the warm crust.

Bake until the filling is just set and barely jiggles in the center, 25–30 minutes. Transfer the baking dish to a wire rack and let cool for about 30 minutes. Use the parchment paper to lift the dessert from the dish. Cut into 16 bars and dust generously with confectioners' sugar.

TIP *An excellent make-ahead dessert for parties, these lemon bars set up more if you chill them. Cover the dish with plastic wrap and refrigerate for up to 3 days before cutting into bars.*

VARIATION

Orange Creamsicle Bars

Make and bake the crust as directed. Make the filling, replacing the lemon zest, lemon juice, and milk with 5 teaspoons grated orange zest, 3 teaspoons grated lemon zest, ¾ cup (180 ml) fresh orange juice, ⅓ cup (80 ml) heavy cream, and 1 teaspoon orange-flower water (optional). Pour the filling on top of the warm crust and bake as directed.

Seven-Layer Bars

You won't need a mixing bowl and spoon to make these buttery, nutty, chocolaty bars. Just layer the ingredients in the dish and bake. If you like, trade out half of the bittersweet chocolate chips for white chocolate chips, or substitute peanut butter chips for the butterscotch chips.

½ cup (4 oz/125 g)
unsalted butter

1½ cups (4½ oz/140 g)
graham cracker crumbs
(about 10 crackers)

1½ cups (9 oz/280 g)
bittersweet chocolate chips

1 cup (6 oz/185 g)
butterscotch chips

1 cup (3 oz/90 g) rolled oats

1 cup (4 oz/125 g) pecans,
toasted and chopped

1 cup (4 oz/125 g) walnuts,
toasted and chopped

1 can (14 fl oz/430 ml)
sweetened condensed milk

1½ cups (6 oz/185 g) shredded
dried unsweetened coconut

MAKES 20 BARS

Preheat the oven to 350°F (180°C).

Put the butter in a 9-by-13-inch (23-by-33-cm) baking dish and transfer to the oven. When the butter has melted, swirl to coat the bottom and sides of the dish.

Spread the graham cracker crumbs in an even layer on the bottom of the dish. Layer the chocolate chips, butterscotch chips, oats, pecans, and walnuts on top. Pour the condensed milk over the entire surface. Sprinkle the coconut on top.

Bake until the coconut is toasted and the edges are golden brown, 20–25 minutes. Transfer the baking dish to a wire rack and let cool completely, then cut into bars.

TIP *To crush the graham crackers, put them in a small food processor and pulse until finely chopped. Or, place them in a lock-top plastic bag, seal it, and gently hit it with a rolling pin to break them up.*

Fudgy Brownies

Rich and dense, these brownies are guaranteed to satisfy any chocolate-lover's sweet tooth. Delicious on their own, they also make the perfect base for a brownie sundae and taste amazing with your favorite dark roast coffee.

1 cup (8 oz/225 g) unsalted butter, plus more for greasing

½ lb (230 g) semisweet chocolate, coarsely chopped

1 cup (7 oz/200 g) granulated sugar

1¼ cups (9½ oz/270 g) firmly packed light brown sugar

4 large eggs, at room temperature, lightly beaten

1½ tablespoons pure vanilla extract

1 cup (4 oz/115 g) all-purpose flour

1 cup (3 oz/90 g) unsweetened Dutch-process cocoa powder

2 teaspoons kosher salt

MAKES ABOUT 24 BROWNIES

Preheat the oven to 350°F (180°C). Grease a 9-by-13-inch (23-by-33-cm) baking dish. Line with parchment paper, letting the paper overhang on two sides by about 1 inch (2.5 cm). Grease the parchment.

Place the butter and ¼ lb (115 g) of the chocolate in a large heatproof bowl set over but not touching barely simmering water in a saucepan and heat, whisking occasionally, until the butter and chocolate melt. Remove from the heat and whisk in both sugars until dissolved. Add the eggs one at a time and whisk until incorporated, then whisk in the vanilla. Sift the flour, cocoa powder, and salt over the chocolate mixture and, using a rubber spatula, fold in until the flour disappears. Fold in the remaining ¼ lb (115 g) chocolate. Transfer the batter to the prepared dish and spread evenly.

Bake until a toothpick inserted into the center of the brownies comes out with only a few moist crumbs attached, 25–30 minutes. Take care not to overbake.

Let cool in the dish for 10 minutes, then use the parchment paper to lift the brownies from the dish and transfer to a cutting board and allow to cool 10 minutes longer. Cut into 24 squares and serve warm or at room temperature.

TIP *This is a very rich fudgy brownie, delicious on its own, but even better as a vessel for ice cream, aka a brownie sundae.*

Brown Butter Goldies

The white chocolate and butterscotch chips pair beautifully with the nutty brown butter in these bars, and a garnish of toasted coconut can be added after baking to bring a lighter note, if you like. Be sure to watch the butter carefully once it starts to turn golden, as it can scorch quickly.

Nonstick cooking spray

1 cup (4 oz/115 g) all-purpose flour

¾ teaspoon kosher salt

½ teaspoon baking powder

⅛ teaspoon baking soda

½ cup (4 oz/115 g) unsalted butter, cut into 8 pieces

1 cup (7½ oz/210 g) firmly packed dark brown sugar

1 large egg

1 teaspoon vanilla bean paste or 2 teaspoons pure vanilla extract

½ cup (3 oz/90 g) white, butterscotch, or semisweet chocolate chips

MAKES 16 BARS

Preheat the oven to 350°F (180°C). Line an 8-inch (20-cm) square baking dish with parchment paper, letting the paper overhang on two opposite sides by about 1 inch (2.5 cm). Lightly coat the parchment with nonstick cooking spray.

In a small bowl, whisk the flour, salt, baking powder, and baking soda. Set aside.

In a small saucepan over medium heat, melt the butter, swirling the pan occasionally, until starting to foam, about 3 minutes. Continue cooking until the butter turns a deep golden color and smells nutty, 5–7 minutes longer. Watch the butter carefully at the end to prevent it from burning. Transfer to a large heatproof bowl and let cool completely, about 15 minutes.

Add the brown sugar to the bowl with the brown butter and stir until thoroughly combined. Add the egg and vanilla and whisk until blended. Add the flour mixture and stir until the flour disappears. The batter will be thick. Using a rubber spatula, fold in the chips. Transfer the batter to the prepared dish and spread evenly.

Bake until the dessert is deep golden brown on top and a toothpick inserted into the center comes out clean, 25–28 minutes.

Let cool in the dish for 10 minutes, then use the parchment paper to lift the dessert from the dish and transfer to a wire rack and allow to cool completely. Cut into 2-inch squares and serve.

S'Mores Brownies

Anyone who lines up for both s'mores and brownies is guaranteed to swoon over these marshmallow-topped graham-cracker-laced brownies. They taste best the day they are baked, but will keep tightly covered at room temperature for up to 3 days. To pack these treats for picnics and potlucks, wrap them individually in aluminum foil or waxed paper.

1 cup (8 oz/250 g) unsalted butter, plus more for greasing

10 oz (315 g) bittersweet chocolate, finely chopped

1 cup (8 oz/250 g) granulated sugar

¾ cup (6 oz/185 g) firmly packed light brown sugar

4 large eggs

2 teaspoons pure vanilla extract

1 teaspoon kosher salt

1⅓ cups (5½ oz/170 g) cake flour

3 tablespoons natural cocoa powder

About 6 graham crackers, roughly crushed with your hands

About 12 jumbo marshmallows

MAKES 12 BROWNIES

Preheat the oven to 350°F (180°C). Generously butter a 9-by-13-inch (23-by-33-cm) baking dish.

In a large saucepan over low heat, combine the butter and chocolate and heat, stirring often, until melted, about 4 minutes. Remove from the heat and whisk in the granulated sugar and brown sugar. Whisk in the eggs one at a time, beating well after each addition. Whisk in the vanilla and salt.

Sift the flour and cocoa powder over the chocolate mixture and, using a rubber spatula, stir in until just blended. Stir in the graham crackers.

Pour the batter into the prepared baking dish and spread evenly. Top evenly with the marshmallows.

Bake until a toothpick inserted into the center comes out almost completely clean, 30–35 minutes. Transfer the dish to a wire rack and let cool completely. Cut into big, gooey squares.

TIP *To make it easier to cut the brownies, fill a tall glass or pitcher with very hot water. Dip your knife in the water and wipe it off with a paper towel before each cut. This technique also works great for cutting cookie bars and frosted layer cakes.*

CAKES

Birthday Cake

This cheerful, rainbow-speckled layer cake is the perfect finale for any kid's birthday party. All you need to transform a buttery yellow cake into a colorful showstopper is a handful of rainbow nonpareils or sprinkles. The marzipan is easy to prepare and cut into fun shapes, but if you want to keep things simple, just decorate the buttercream with more rainbow sprinkles!

1 recipe Marzipan (page 222; made with food colorings of your choice)

1 recipe Yellow Cake (page 220)

1 cup (5 oz/160 g) wax-coated rainbow sprinkles, plus more for decorating

1 recipe Vanilla Buttercream (page 223)

SERVES 12

Make the marzipan and refrigerate as directed.

Preheat the oven, prepare the pans, and make the yellow cake batter as directed. Remove the bowl from the mixer and, using a rubber spatula, fold in the sprinkles.

Divide the batter evenly between the prepared pans and spread evenly. Bake until a toothpick inserted into the center of the cakes comes out clean, about 55 minutes. Transfer the pans to wire racks and let cool for 10 minutes, then invert the cakes onto the racks and let cool completely.

Roll out the marzipan dough ½ inch (12 mm) thick and cut out triangles. Make the vanilla buttercream.

To assemble the cake, using a large serrated knife, cut each cake in half horizontally to create 4 thin layers. Place the bottom layer cut side down on a cake stand or serving plate. Using an offset spatula, spread about one-fourth of the buttercream evenly over the cake. Repeat with the remaining layers. Spread the top and sides of the cake with a very thin layer of buttercream and refrigerate for 30 minutes. Spread the remaining buttercream over the top and sides of the chilled cake. Cover the entire top of the cake with sprinkles. Arrange the marzipan triangles next to each other around the sides of the cake to form a banner, pressing gently to adhere. Cut into slices and serve.

TIP *For an exceptionally colorful cake, use small pearled sprinkles. For a more controlled speckled effect, use sprinkles like those you'd find in an ice cream shop.*

KIDS AT HEART
Adults will love this festive celebration cake just as much as little ones do.

FINISHING TOUCH
The "naked cake" effect on this modern carrot cake sets it apart from a more traditional presentation.

Carrot Cake with Cream Cheese Frosting

Take classic carrot cake to the next level by transforming it into a triple-layer treat made moist with crushed pineapple, then embellished with cream cheese frosting and toasty walnuts. Using real carrots "buried" in the frosting is an easy way to add a bit of whimsy to the decoration.

FOR THE CAKE

¾ cup (180 ml) canola oil, plus more for greasing

2¼ cups (11½ oz/360 g) all-purpose flour, plus more for dusting

2 teaspoons baking soda

2 teaspoons kosher salt

5 teaspoons ground cinnamon

2 teaspoons ground ginger

¼ teaspoon ground nutmeg

⅛ teaspoon ground cloves

3 large eggs

2¼ cups (18 oz/560 g) sugar

¾ cup (180 ml) buttermilk

2 teaspoons pure vanilla extract

6 oz (185 g) crushed pineapple, drained

3 cups (15 oz/470 g) grated peeled carrots

1 recipe Cream Cheese Frosting (page 225)

3 carrots, with tops attached

½ cup (2 oz/60 g) chopped toasted walnuts

SERVES 16

To make the cake, preheat the oven to 350°F (180°C). Grease three 9-inch (23-cm) round cake pans, line the bottoms of the pans with parchment paper, then grease the parchment. Dust with flour, then tap out any excess.

In a large bowl, sift together the flour, baking soda, salt, cinnamon, ginger, nutmeg, and cloves. Set aside.

In the bowl of a stand mixer fitted with the paddle attachment, beat together the eggs, sugar, oil, buttermilk, and vanilla on low speed until smooth, about 1 minute. Add the flour mixture in 2 additions and beat until combined, about 1 minute. Add the pineapple and grated carrots and beat until just incorporated.

Divide the batter evenly among the prepared pans and spread evenly. Bake until the tops of the cakes are browned and shiny and a toothpick inserted into the center comes out clean, 25–30 minutes. Transfer the pans to wire racks and let cool for 10 minutes, then invert the cakes onto the racks and let cool completely.

Make the cream cheese frosting.

To assemble the cake, place 1 cake layer on a cake stand or serving plate. Spread one-third of the cream cheese frosting evenly over the cake. Repeat with the remaining cake layers, including the top layer. Using an offset spatula, spread a thin layer of frosting on all sides of the cake to create a "naked" cake effect. Carefully peel the carrots, keeping the tops intact. Gently press the carrots into the top of the cake in varying depths. Scatter the walnuts around the carrots and serve.

Cookies & Cream Cupcakes

Transform simple chocolate cupcakes into an all-time favorite ice cream flavor: cookies and cream. By sandwiching luscious cream cheese frosting, flecked with chocolate cookie crumbs, between a cupcake's layers, it even looks like a chocolate cream sandwich cookie.

2 cups (10 oz/315 g) all-purpose flour

1 cup (3 oz/90 g) unsweetened cocoa powder

1 teaspoon baking powder

1 teaspoon baking soda

½ teaspoon kosher salt

2 cups (1 lb/500 g) sugar

1 cup (250 ml) canola oil

2 large eggs

1 tablespoon pure vanilla extract

1 cup (8 oz/250 g) sour cream

1 recipe Cream Cheese Frosting (page 225)

1¼ cups (3¾ oz/110 g) chocolate cookie crumbs (cream filling removed)

12 chocolate sandwich cookies, broken in half, for toppings

MAKES 24 CUPCAKES

Place 1 rack in the upper third and 1 rack in the lower third of the oven and preheat to 350°F (180°C). Line 24 standard muffin cups with paper liners. In a bowl, sift together the flour, cocoa powder, baking powder, baking soda, and salt. Set aside.

In the bowl of a stand mixer fitted with the paddle attachment, beat together the sugar, oil, eggs, vanilla, and ½ cup (125 ml) water on medium speed until combined. Reduce the speed and add the flour mixture in 3 additions, alternating with the sour cream and beginning and ending with the flour, and beat until combined.

Divide the batter among the prepared muffin cups, filling them three-fourths full. (Don't fill less than three-fourths full because you want the cupcakes to form a dome when baking.) Bake until the tops of the cupcakes have formed a crust but still spring back when lightly touched and a toothpick inserted into the center comes out clean, 20–25 minutes, rotating the pans between the racks halfway through baking. Transfer the pans to wire racks and let cool for 10 minutes. Remove the cupcakes from the pans and let cool completely on the racks.

Make the cream cheese frosting. After beating in the cream, add the cookie crumbs and beat until well combined, about 30 seconds. Transfer to a large pastry bag fitted with a large closed star tip.

Slice off the cupcake tops right where they meet the paper liners and reserve the cake tops. Pipe a layer of frosting around the outside edge of each cupcake, then cover with a reserved cupcake top. Pipe a dollop of frosting in the center of each cupcake, top with a cookie piece, and serve.

PARTY WORTHY

These sculptural cupcakes are an impressive finale for any celebration.

Flourless Chocolate & Hazelnut Fallen Cake

When baked, this flourless dark chocolate cake puffs up almost like a soufflé, then gently falls and cracks as it cools, leaving a delightfully crisp crust and a tender, rich interior. It also leaves a hollow in the center of the cake, perfect for filling with Frangelico-scented whipped cream, toasty chopped hazelnuts, and pretty chocolate shavings.

½ cup (4 oz/125 g) unsalted butter, cut into cubes, plus more for greasing

¾ cup (6 oz/185 g) granulated sugar, plus more for dusting

10 oz (315 g) semisweet chocolate, chopped

2 tablespoons canola oil

4 large eggs, separated, plus 2 large eggs

2 tablespoons Frangelico

2 tablespoons unsweetened cocoa powder

1 teaspoon pure vanilla extract

1 teaspoon kosher salt

¾ cup (2¾ oz/75 g) finely ground hazelnuts

1 recipe Frangelico Whipped Cream (page 225)

Chopped toasted hazelnuts, for garnish

Shaved chocolate, for garnish

SERVES 8–10

Preheat the oven to 350°F (180°C). Grease a 9-inch (23-cm) springform pan, line the bottom of the pan with parchment paper, then grease the parchment. Dust with granulated sugar, then tap out any excess.

Combine the butter, chocolate, and oil in a large heatproof bowl and set over but not touching barely simmering water in a saucepan. Heat, stirring occasionally, until melted and smooth, about 4 minutes. Remove the bowl from the heat.

In the bowl of a stand mixer fitted with the whisk attachment, beat the egg whites on medium-high speed until frothy, about 1 minute. Add ½ cup (4 oz/125 g) of the granulated sugar and beat until stiff peaks form, about 3 minutes. Set aside.

In a medium bowl, whisk together the egg yolks, eggs, Frangelico, the remaining ¼ cup (2 oz/60 g) granulated sugar, cocoa powder, vanilla, and salt until smooth. Add the egg yolk mixture to the chocolate mixture and whisk until incorporated, about 1 minute. Fold one-fourth of the egg whites and all of the ground hazelnuts into the chocolate mixture, then gently fold in the remaining egg whites until uniformly combined.

Pour the batter into the prepared pan and spread evenly. Bake until the cake has risen above the rim of the pan and is set on top, 35–40 minutes. Transfer the pan to a wire rack and let cool completely. The cake will fall slightly and crack on top as it cools.

Make the Frangelico whipped cream. Remove the outer ring of the pan. Mound the whipped cream in the center of the cake and garnish with chopped hazelnuts and shaved chocolate.

Red Velvet Cake with Cream Cheese Frosting

Red velvet cake originally got its name from the moist, velvety texture and subtle red hue created by the reaction between buttermilk, cocoa powder, and vinegar. For a kid's birthday party, decorate the cake with rainbow sprinkles on top of the cake and colorful marzipan shapes around the base.

½ cup (4 oz/125 g) unsalted butter, at room temperature, plus more for greasing

2½ cups (12½ oz/390 g) all-purpose flour, plus more for dusting

¼ cup (¾ oz/20 g) unsweetened cocoa powder

1 teaspoon each baking powder and kosher salt

1½ cups (375 ml) buttermilk

2 tablespoons red food coloring

2 cups (1 lb/500 g) sugar

2 large eggs

2 teaspoons pure vanilla extract

1½ teaspoons baking soda

1 tablespoon distilled white vinegar

1 recipe Cream Cheese Frosting (page 225)

SERVES 12

Preheat the oven to 350°F (180°C). Grease two 8-inch (20-cm) round cake pans, line the bottoms of the pans with parchment paper, then grease the parchment. Dust with flour, then tap out any excess.

In a bowl, sift together the flour, cocoa powder, baking powder, and salt. In a small bowl, whisk together the buttermilk and food coloring. Set aside.

In the bowl of a stand mixer fitted with the paddle attachment, beat together the butter and sugar on medium speed until light and fluffy, about 2 minutes. Add the eggs one at a time and then the vanilla and beat until incorporated, about 1 minute. Reduce the speed to low and add the flour mixture in 3 additions, alternating with the buttermilk and beginning and ending with the flour, and beat until combined. In a small bowl, whisk together the baking soda and vinegar. When the fizzing subsides, use a rubber spatula to fold it into the batter.

Divide the batter evenly between the prepared pans. Bake until a toothpick inserted into the center of the cakes comes out clean, 35–40 minutes. Transfer the pans to wire racks and let cool for 10 minutes, then invert the cakes onto the racks and let cool completely.

Make the cream cheese frosting. To assemble the cake, place 1 cake layer on a serving plate. Spread about one-third of the frosting onto the top of the cake and spread evenly with an offset spatula. Place the other layer on top. Cover the entire cake with a thin layer of frosting and refrigerate for 30 minutes. Working with the chilled cake, spread the remaining cream cheese frosting on the top and sides of the cake.

TOUCH OF SWEETNESS
This cake is a lovely balance of rich honey and tart sour cream. To make it sweeter, add an additional 1 cup (4 oz/125 g) confectioners' sugar to the frosting.

8-Layer Honey-Pistachio Cake

This sweet, impressive cake—which hails from Russia—has eight delicate, honey-infused layers that are made from a cookie-like dough. Once rolled, cut, and baked, the layers are sandwiched with a mixture of whipped cream and sour cream, which softens them to a melt-in-your-mouth texture. A dusting of pistachios adds both color and texture to the top of the cake.

FOR THE CAKE

3 cups (15 oz/470 g) all-purpose flour, plus more for dusting

1 teaspoon baking soda

¼ teaspoon kosher salt

½ cup (6 oz/185 g) honey

½ cup (4 oz/125 g) granulated sugar

2 tablespoons unsalted butter

3 large eggs

FOR THE SOUR CREAM FROSTING

1 cup (250 ml) heavy cream

4 cups (2 lb/1 kg) sour cream

2 cups (8 oz/250 g) confectioners' sugar

1 teaspoon pure vanilla extract

¼ teaspoon kosher salt

½ cup (2 oz/60 g) toasted pistachios, crushed

SERVES 12

To make the cake, preheat the oven to 350°F (180°C). Line a baking sheet with parchment paper.

In a bowl, sift together the flour, baking soda, and salt. Set aside. In a large saucepan over medium heat, combine the honey, granulated sugar, and butter and cook, stirring occasionally, until the butter melts and the sugar and honey dissolve, about 5 minutes. Remove from the heat and let cool slightly.

In a small bowl, whisk the eggs until blended. Add a small amount of the honey mixture to the eggs and whisk to combine. While whisking constantly, gradually add the egg mixture to the honey mixture in the saucepan. Using a rubber spatula, fold in the flour mixture until almost incorporated, then transfer to a lightly floured surface and knead just to form a disk. Divide the disk into 8 equal pieces.

Roll out each piece of dough into a 9-inch (23-cm) round. Using an 8-inch (20-cm) plate or cake pan for tracing, cut each piece into an 8-inch (20-cm) round, reserving the scraps. Transfer 2 rounds to the prepared baking sheet and bake until crisp and golden brown, about 6 minutes. Transfer to a wire rack and let cool. Repeat with the remaining rounds. The cooled rounds should have the texture of graham crackers. Place the reserved dough scraps in a single layer on the baking sheet and bake until crisp and golden brown, about 6 minutes. Set aside.

To make the sour cream frosting, in the bowl of a stand mixer fitted with the whisk attachment, beat the cream on medium-high speed until stiff peaks form, about 3 minutes. In a large bowl, using a handheld whisk, whisk together the sour cream, confectioners' sugar, vanilla, and salt. Using a rubber spatula, fold in the whipped cream.

To assemble the cake, place 1 cake round on a parchment-lined baking sheet or a cake circle. Spread about ½ cup (125 ml) of the sour cream frosting evenly over the disk, all the way to the edges (it's okay if some spills over). Top with another cake round and spread with frosting, then repeat with the remaining cake rounds. Spread the remaining frosting evenly over the top and sides of the cake. Using a small food processor, or a plastic bag and a rolling pin, crush the scrap pieces. Press the crumbs onto the sides of the cake. Sprinkle the pistachios over the top.

Refrigerate the cake overnight; the frosting will soften the layers into a cakelike texture. Serve chilled or at room temperature.

Chocolate Almond Cake with Poached Pears

Pears poached in amaretto are a tasty dessert in their own right, but serve slices of the sweet poached fruit atop dark chocolate cake layered with mascarpone whipped cream and the result is truly magnificent.

1 recipe Amaretto-Poached Pears (page 222)

1 recipe Almond-Mascarpone Whipped Cream (page 110)

FOR THE CAKE

¾ cup (6 oz/185 g) unsalted butter, at room temperature, plus more for greasing

2 cups (10 oz/315 g) all-purpose flour, plus more for dusting

6 oz (185 g) semisweet chocolate

½ cup (125 ml) whole milk

¾ cup (6 oz/185 g) each granulated sugar and firmly packed light brown sugar

3 tablespoons unsweetened cocoa powder

2 teaspoons baking powder

¾ teaspoon kosher salt

3 large eggs

1 teaspoon pure vanilla extract

⅓ cup (2½ oz/75 g) sour cream

SERVES 12

Make the amaretto-poached pears and almond-mascarpone whipped cream as directed. Cover and refrigerate until ready to use.

To make the cake, preheat the oven to 325°F (165°C). Grease two 8-inch (20-cm) round cake pans, line the bottoms of the pans with parchment paper, then grease the parchment. Dust with flour, then tap out any excess.

Combine the butter, chocolate, and milk in a heatproof bowl and set over but not touching barely simmering water in a saucepan. Heat, stirring occasionally, until melted, about 8 minutes. Remove from the heat and whisk to combine. Set aside.

In a large bowl, sift together the flour, both sugars, cocoa powder, baking powder, and salt. Whisk in the eggs and vanilla. Whisk the sour cream into the chocolate mixture, then add to the flour mixture and whisk until completely incorporated. Divide the batter evenly among the prepared pans. Bake until a toothpick inserted into the center of the cakes comes out clean, 35–40 minutes. Transfer the pans to wire racks and let cool for 10 minutes, then invert the cakes onto the racks and let cool completely.

To assemble the cake, place 1 cake layer on a cake stand or serving plate. Spread half of the almond-mascarpone whipped cream evenly over the cake, then top with the other cake layer. Spread the remaining whipped cream, except for ¼ cup (60 ml), evenly over the cake. Using an offset spatula, spread the reserved whipped cream in a very thin layer on the sides to create a "naked" cake effect. Refrigerate until set, about 20 minutes.

Arrange the pears on top of the cake. If desired, pour the poaching liquid through a fine-mesh sieve and drizzle over the top. Serve.

FANCY FINISH
Embellish the cake with
a liberal sprinkling of lightly
toasted sliced almonds.

STAR OF THE PARTY
These pretty mini cakes are a welcome guest at an afternoon tea party, bridal shower, or any fancy fête.

Champagne & Raspberry Mini Layer Cakes

These elegant layer cakes shine with the addition of sparkling wine and raspberry purée. There's no need to use expensive champagne, but use a sparkling wine that you'd like to drink and serve glasses of it alongside the cakes.

Unsalted butter, for greasing

All-purpose flour, for dusting

1 recipe Champagne Cake (page 219)

½ recipe Raspberry Filling (page 220)

FOR THE CHAMPAGNE BUTTERCREAM

1 cup (8 oz/250 g) unsalted butter, at room temperature

4 cups (1 lb/500 g) confectioners' sugar

5 tablespoons (80 ml) sparkling wine

1 teaspoon pure vanilla extract

¼ teaspoon kosher salt

⅓ cup (1 oz/20 g) freeze-dried raspberries

⅓ cup (1½ oz/45 g) fresh raspberries

MAKES THREE 3-INCH (7.5-CM) 3-LAYER CAKES; SERVES 6

Preheat the oven to 350°F (180°C). Grease a rimmed sheet cake pan, line the pan with parchment paper, then grease the parchment. Dust with flour, then tap out any excess. Make the champagne cake batter.

Spread the batter in the prepared pan. Bake until a toothpick inserted into the center of the cake comes out clean, about 25 minutes. Let cool completely in the pan on a wire rack, then invert the cake onto a cutting board or an upside-down baking sheet. Remove the parchment. Using a 3-inch (7.5-cm) round cutter, cut out 9 rounds.

Make the raspberry filling.

To make the buttercream, in the bowl of a stand mixer fitted with the paddle attachment, beat the butter on medium speed until smooth, about 2 minutes. Add the confectioners' sugar, sparkling wine, vanilla, and salt, raise the speed to medium-high, and beat until combined, stopping the mixer to scrape down the sides of the bowl as needed.

To assemble the cakes, transfer one-fourth of the buttercream to a pastry bag and cut a ½-inch (12-mm) opening. Pipe a ring around the outside edge of 1 cake round, then spread a layer of raspberry filling in the center. Top with another cake round and repeat to form 3 cake layers. Repeat to assemble the remaining cakes.

Refrigerate the cakes until set, about 1 hour. Spread the remaining buttercream over the tops and sides of the cakes. Garnish with freeze-dried and fresh raspberries and serve.

TIP *If the buttercream is too loose, add more confectioners' sugar. If it is too thick, stir in more sparkling wine or a few teaspoons of milk.*

Lemon Genoise Cake with Meringue Frosting

This swoon-worthy dessert is a riff on lemon meringue pie, featuring three lemony cake layers spread with lemon curd and fluffy meringue frosting. Use a kitchen torch to easily toast the meringue to a golden brown hue.

1 recipe Lemon Curd (page 222)

½ cup (2½ oz/75 g) all-purpose flour

½ cup (2 oz/60 g) cornstarch

9 large eggs, separated, plus 1 large egg

1 cup (8 oz/250 g) sugar

1½ tablespoons grated lemon zest

¾ cup (6 oz/185 g) unsalted butter, melted and cooled

1 recipe Meringue Frosting (page 225)

SERVES 12

Make the lemon curd and refrigerate as directed.

Preheat the oven to 325°F (165°C). In a bowl, sift together the flour and cornstarch. Set aside.

In the bowl of a stand mixer fitted with the whisk attachment, beat together the egg yolks and egg on medium speed until combined. Raise the speed to medium-high, slowly add ½ cup (4 oz/125 g) of the sugar, and beat until the mixture is pale and has tripled in volume, 3–5 minutes. Transfer the egg yolk mixture to a bowl and set aside.

In the clean bowl of the stand mixer fitted with the clean whisk attachment, beat the egg whites on medium speed until foamy. Raise the speed to medium-high, slowly add the remaining ½ cup (4 oz/125 g) sugar, and beat until stiff peaks form, 3–5 minutes. Remove the bowl from the mixer and, using a rubber spatula, carefully fold the egg yolk mixture into the egg white mixture. (This is the opposite of the usual technique, but it's correct.) Add the lemon zest. Sift the flour mixture over the egg mixture and fold until the flour streaks begin to disappear. Add the melted butter and fold until just combined.

Divide the batter evenly among three ungreased 8-inch (20-cm) round cake pans or two 9-inch (23-cm) cake pans and spread evenly. Bake until the cakes spring back when lightly touched and a toothpick inserted into the center comes out with just a few moist crumbs attached, about 30 minutes. Transfer the pans to wire racks, let cool for 10 minutes, then invert the cakes onto a rack and let cool completely.

To assemble the cake, place 1 cake layer on a cake stand. Spread half of the lemon curd over the cake. Top with a second cake layer and spread the remaining lemon curd over the cake. Top with the third cake layer and refrigerate while you prepare the meringue.

Make the meringue frosting. Fill a large pastry bag fitted with an open star tip with the meringue, being careful not to deflate the meringue. Pipe florets along the bottom and up the sides, finishing on the top. Using a kitchen torch, toast the meringue until nicely browned. Though the frosting is best when used right away, it can be covered and refrigerated for to up to 1 day. Beat again before using.

TIP *Keep in mind that this batter will deflate if not used right away.*

SWIRLS OF BEAUTY

The meringue florets that adorn this naturally leavened cake are created using an open star piping tip.

HIDDEN FLAVORS
A combination of coconut milk and extract transform traditional buttercream for this chic celebration cake.

Coconut & Lime Curd Layer Cake

Coconut layer cake, split and filled with lemon or lime curd and slathered with fluffy 7-minute frosting and a blizzard of shredded coconut, is a mainstay of the Southern kitchen. We've updated this classic with our moist buttermilk cake, homemade lime curd, and coconut buttercream, topped with a flurry of colorful flowers and finely grated lime zest.

1 recipe Lime Curd (page 222)

1 recipe Coconut Buttercream (page 223)

FOR THE CAKE

1 cup (8 oz/250 g) plus 2 tablespoons unsalted butter, at room temperature, plus more for greasing

4 cups (1¼ lb/625 g) plus 2 tablespoons all-purpose flour, plus more for dusting

3¾ teaspoons baking powder

1⅛ teaspoons baking soda

1⅛ teaspoons kosher salt

4 large egg whites plus 2 large eggs

3 cups (1½ lb/750 g) sugar

1½ tablespoons pure vanilla extract

2¼ cups (560 ml) buttermilk

Edible flowers and grated lime zest, for garnish

SERVES 18

Make the lime curd and coconut buttercream. Cover and refrigerate until ready to use or for up to three days.

To make the cake, preheat the oven to 350°F (180°C). Grease three 8-inch (20-cm) round cake pans, line the bottoms of the pans with parchment paper, then grease the parchment. Dust with flour, then tap out any excess.

In a bowl, sift together the flour, baking powder, baking soda, and salt. Set aside.

In the bowl of the stand mixer fitted with the whisk attachment, beat together the egg whites and 1 cup (8 oz/250 g) of the sugar on medium-high speed until soft peaks form, about 5 minutes. Set aside.

In the clean bowl of the stand mixer fitted with the paddle attachment, beat together the butter and the remaining 2 cups (1 lb/500 g) sugar on medium speed until light and fluffy, about 2 minutes. Add the eggs one at a time and vanilla and beat until incorporated, about 1 minute. Stop the mixer and scrape down the sides of the bowl. With the mixer on low speed, add the flour mixture in 3 additions, alternating with the buttermilk and beginning and ending with the flour and beat until combined. Stop the mixer and scrape down the sides of the bowl. Raise the speed to high and beat for 20 seconds.

Using a rubber spatula, gently fold the egg whites into the butter mixture until completely incorporated, taking care not to deflate the peaks.

Divide the batter evenly among the prepared pans and spread evenly. Bake until a toothpick inserted into the center of the cakes comes out clean, 40–45 minutes. Transfer the pans to wire racks and let cool for 10 minutes, then invert the cakes onto the racks and let cool completely.

Transfer one-fourth of the buttercream to a pastry bag and cut a ½-inch (12-mm) opening.

To assemble the cake, place 1 cake layer, top side up, on a cake stand or serving plate. Pipe a ring of buttercream around the edge of the cake, then fill the center with half of the lime curd. Top with a second cake layer, pipe a ring of buttercream, and fill the center with the remaining lime curd. Top with the third cake layer and spread the remaining buttercream over the top. If desired, reserve a small amount of buttercream and spread a thin layer on the sides to create a "naked" cake effect.

Garnish the cake with edible flowers and lime zest and serve.

Cherry-Olive Oil Cake

Rich with pungent extra-virgin olive oil, this tender cake is a natural partner to lightly sweetened cherry compote. Use fresh cherries at the peak of their season, and choose frozen cherries other times of the year. A dollop of lightly whipped cream is the natural accompaniment.

FOR THE CAKE

1 cup (250 ml) extra-virgin olive oil, plus more for greasing

2 cups (10 oz/315 g) all-purpose flour, sifted

1 cup (8 oz/250 g) granulated sugar

1 cup (7 oz/220 g) firmly packed light brown sugar

1 teaspoon baking powder

1 teaspoon kosher salt

1 cup (250 ml) whole milk

3 large eggs

Zest of 1 lemon

1½ cups (9 oz/280 g) pitted fresh or thawed frozen cherries

FOR THE CHERRY COMPOTE

1½ cups (9 oz/280 g) pitted fresh or thawed frozen cherries

½ cup (3½ oz/105 g) firmly packed light brown sugar

Juice of 1 lemon

Confectioners' sugar, for dusting

SERVES 12

To make the cake, preheat the oven to 350°F (180°C). Grease a 9-inch (23-cm) round cake pan, line the bottom of the pan with parchment paper, then grease the parchment.

In a medium bowl, whisk together the flour, both sugars, baking powder, and salt. In a large bowl, whisk together the oil, milk, eggs, and lemon zest, then stir in the flour mixture until combined. Using a rubber spatula, fold in the cherries.

Pour the batter into the prepared pan and spread evenly. Bake until a toothpick inserted into the center of the cake comes out clean, about 1 hour. Transfer the pan to a wire rack and let cool for 10 minutes, then invert the cake onto the rack and let cool completely.

Meanwhile, make the cherry compote: In a saucepan over medium heat, combine the cherries, brown sugar, and lemon juice and bring to a simmer. Cook, stirring occasionally, until thickened, about 10 minutes. Let cool to room temperature before serving. The compote can be stored in an airtight container in the refrigerator for up to 1 week.

Just before serving, dust the cake with confectioners' sugar and top with the cherry compote.

Gluten-Free Almond & Orange Blossom Cake

Flavored with orange zest, vanilla bean, and orange blossom water, this moist, tender cake has enough fragrant flavor to stand on its own, but add a dollop of whipped cream and a smattering of blackberries to individual portions before serving, if you like. Seek out a good-quality gluten-free flour mix, like Cup4Cup.

Butter for greasing

1 cup (5 oz/140 g) gluten-free flour, plus more for dusting

1 cup (3 oz/90 g) almond meal

1 teaspoon baking powder

½ teaspoon kosher salt

4 large eggs, separated

1½ cups (12 oz/375 g) granulated sugar

Zest of 1 orange

1 tablespoon orange blossom water

1 teaspoon pure vanilla extract

½ teaspoon almond extract

1 vanilla bean, split and seeds scraped, seeds reserved

Confectioners' sugar, for dusting

SERVES 12

Preheat the oven to 350°F (180°C). Grease a 9-inch (23-cm) springform pan, line the bottom of the pan with parchment paper, then grease the parchment. Lightly dust the pan with gluten-free flour or confectioners' sugar, then tap out any excess.

In a bowl, whisk together the gluten-free flour, almond meal, baking powder, and salt. Set aside.

In the bowl of a stand mixer fitted with the whisk attachment, beat together the egg yolks and 1 cup (8 oz/250 g) of the sugar on medium speed until pale yellow and thick, about 3 minutes. Stop the mixer and add the orange zest, orange blossom water, vanilla and almond extracts, and vanilla bean seeds. Beat on medium-high speed until combined, about 1 minute. Transfer to a large bowl and set aside.

In the clean bowl of the stand mixer fitted with the clean whisk attachment, beat the egg whites on medium-high speed until soft peaks form, about 3 minutes. With the mixer running, slowly add the remaining ½ cup (4 oz/125 g) sugar and beat until stiff peaks form, about 2 minutes.

Using a rubber spatula, fold half of the flour mixture into the yolk mixture until combined, then gently fold in half of the egg white mixture until combined, taking care not to deflate the peaks. Fold in the remaining flour and then the remaining egg whites.

Transfer the batter to the prepared pan. Bake until a toothpick inserted into the center of the cake comes out clean, about 45 minutes. Transfer the pan to a wire rack and let cool slightly for 10 minutes, then run an offset spatula around the edges and remove the outer ring of the pan. Dust the cake with confectioners' sugar and serve warm or at room temperature.

Pavlova with Whipped Cream & Berries

The fruit topping is the star of the show, turning this light-as-air dessert into a crowd-pleasing meringue cake. If ripe fresh berries are unavailable, sliced stone fruit and tropical fruit make a colorful variation. When in doubt, choose your region's best in-season produce.

4 large egg whites, at room temperature

1 tablespoon cornstarch, sifted

1 cup (7 oz/200 g) plus 3 tablespoons sugar

2 teaspoons pure vanilla extract

1 teaspoon fresh lemon juice

3 cups (12 oz/340 g) mixed fresh berries, such as strawberries, blueberries, blackberries, and raspberries

1½ cups (350 ml) heavy cream

SERVES 6–8

Place a rack in the lower third of the oven and preheat to 250°F (120°C). Draw a 9-inch (23-cm) circle on a sheet of parchment paper. Turn the parchment over and place on a baking sheet.

In the bowl of a stand mixer fitted with the whisk attachment, beat the egg whites on medium speed until well combined, about 1 minute. Sprinkle the cornstarch over the whites and beat until foamy, about 3 minutes. Raise the speed to high, very gradually add the 1 cup (7 oz/200 g) sugar, and beat until stiff, shiny peaks form, 8–10 minutes. Quickly beat in 1 teaspoon of the vanilla and the lemon juice.

Spread the meringue inside the circle on the parchment paper. Using the back of a large spoon, create an indentation in the center of the meringue and a slight rim around the edges.

Bake until the meringue is crisp and the color has deepened slightly, about 1 hour. Turn off the oven, leave the door closed, and let the meringue cool in the oven for at least 2 hours or up to overnight. Carefully remove the meringue from the parchment paper and place on a serving platter.

In a bowl, stir together the berries and 1 tablespoon of the sugar. Set aside.

In the clean bowl of the stand mixer fitted with the clean whisk attachment, beat together the cream and the remaining 2 tablespoons sugar and 1 teaspoon vanilla on medium speed until soft peaks form, about 4 minutes. Spoon the whipped cream into the hollow of the meringue and top with the berries. Cut the pavlova into wedges and serve.

IN BLOOM

A last-minute sprinkling
of edible spring blooms add
a touch of elegance to this
creative crepe confection.

Dulce de Leche Crepe Cake

By layering lots of thin, eggy crepes with dulce de leche–flavored whipped cream, then topping the whole thing off with dulce de leche sauce, you end up with a gorgeous dessert fit for the most decadent of fêtes. Double the recipe for a magnificently tall cake.

FOR THE CREPES

9 large eggs

1½ cups (12 oz/375 ml) whole milk

1½ cups (7½ oz/235 g) all-purpose flour

¼ cup (1 oz/30 g) plus 1 tablespoon confectioners' sugar

1 tablespoon pure vanilla extract

1½ teaspoons kosher salt

FOR THE DULCE DE LECHE WHIPPED CREAM

1 cup (8 oz/250 g) plus 2 tablespoons granulated sugar

6 tablespoons (3 oz/90 g) cold unsalted butter, cut into small pieces

1½ cups (12 oz/375 ml) evaporated milk

3 cups (24 oz/750 ml) heavy cream

SERVES 8-10

To make the crepes, in a blender, combine the eggs, milk, flour, confectioners' sugar, vanilla, and salt and blend until well combined, about 45 seconds. Stop the blender and scrape down the sides of the bowl, then blend for 30 seconds longer.

Line a baking sheet with parchment paper. Heat a 10-inch (25-cm) crepe pan or nonstick frying pan over medium-low heat (do not grease the pan). Ladle about ¼ cup (60 ml) of the batter into the center of the pan, then quickly lift and rotate the pan to spread the batter to the edges. If the batter begins to set before spreading, reduce the heat. Cook until the crepe is almost completely cooked through, about 2 minutes. Using a rubber spatula and your fingers, carefully flip the crepe over and cook for 15 seconds longer. Transfer the crepe to the prepared baking sheet to cool. Repeat with the remaining batter, stacking the crepes on top of each other. Let the crepes cool completely before assembling the cake.

To make the dulce de leche, prepare an ice water bath in a large bowl. Put the granulated sugar in a large saucepan, place over medium-high heat, and stir until the sugar begins to melt. Continue stirring, breaking up clumps of sugar as they form, until all of the sugar has melted and turned a golden caramel color, 8–10 minutes. Add the butter (the mixture will start to bubble) and stir until the butter has melted. While stirring constantly, slowly stir in the evaporated milk (the mixture will continue to bubble) and cook, stirring occasionally, until the mixture is bubbling toward the top of the pan and has formed a cohesive caramel-like texture, about 5 minutes. Place the saucepan in the ice bath and stir until the sauce is cool to the touch, then let stand at room temperature to cool completely.

In the bowl of a stand mixer fitted with the whisk attachment, beat the cream on medium-high speed until soft peaks form, about 3 minutes. Remove the bowl from the mixer. Using a rubber spatula, fold in about half of the dulce de leche until fully incorporated. Reserve the remaining dulce de leche for drizzling over the cake.

To assemble the cake, place 1 crepe on a cake stand or serving plate. Top with a generous dollop of the dulce de leche whipped cream and spread evenly over the crepe. Repeat with the remaining crepes and whipped cream. Refrigerate until ready to serve. Just before serving, heat the remaining dulce de leche over low heat until slightly loosened but not hot. Pour over the cake and let drizzle down the sides. The cake can be stored in an airtight container at room temperature for up to 2 days.

TIP *For a 40-layer cake, double the crepe batter recipe. Double the dulce de leche whipped cream recipe and assemble as directed.*

Chocolate Espresso Heart Cake

You don't need a special pan to create a heart-shaped cake for your Valentine. Here, we show you how to use round and square cake pans to make a scrumptious espresso-infused chocolate cake in the shape of a heart. A thick layer of frosting and plenty of edible flowers or sprinkles provide the finishing touch.

FOR THE CAKE

½ cup (125 ml) canola oil, plus more for greasing

2½ cups (12½ oz/390 g) all-purpose flour, plus more for dusting

1 cup (3 oz/90 g) unsweetened cocoa powder

1½ teaspoons each baking powder, baking soda, and kosher salt

2 cups (1 lb/500 g) sugar

3 large eggs

1½ cups (375 ml) buttermilk

1 tablespoon pure vanilla extract

6 oz (185 g) semisweet chocolate chips, melted and cooled

4 teaspoons espresso powder

FROSTING OPTIONS

For a pink cake: 1 recipe Vanilla Buttercream (page 223), tinted with red food coloring

For a double chocolate cake: 1 recipe Chocolate Frosting (page 223)

Edible flowers or rainbow sprinkles, for decorating

SERVES 12–16

To make the cake, preheat the oven to 350°F (180°C). Grease an 8-inch (20-cm) round cake pan and an 8-inch (20-cm) square cake pan, line the bottoms of the pans with parchment paper, then grease the parchment. Dust with flour, then tap out any excess.

In a bowl, sift together the flour, cocoa powder, baking powder, baking soda, and salt. Set aside.

In the bowl of a stand mixer fitted with the paddle attachment, beat together the sugar, eggs, buttermilk, oil, and vanilla on medium speed until blended, about 2 minutes. Reduce the speed to low, slowly add the flour mixture, and beat until incorporated, stopping the mixer to scrape down the sides of the bowl as needed. Add the melted chocolate and espresso powder and beat until combined. Raise the speed to high and beat for 30 seconds.

Divide the batter evenly between the prepared pans and spread evenly. Bake until a toothpick inserted into the center of the cakes comes out clean, 30–35 minutes. Transfer the pans to wire racks and let cool for 10 minutes, then invert the cakes onto the racks and let cool completely.

To assemble, cut the round cake in half crosswise. Orient the square cake as a diamond. Frost the cut sides of the half rounds with buttercream or chocolate frosting and place them against the top sides of the diamond to form a heart shape, pressing gently to adhere. Spread the remaining buttercream or frosting over the entire surface of the cake. Decorate as desired with edible flowers or sprinkles and serve.

EXPRESS YOURSELF
Reserve some of the frosting
to pipe an extra sweet
message to your valentine.

CHRISTMAS CLASSIC
With their wintry scenes, these festive log-shaped cakes are a holiday favorite.

Bûche de Noël

This traditional holiday cake is created from a chocolate and whipped cream roulade, or rolled cake, decorated to look like a log. The finished cake takes some time, but it makes a fun family project. The little marzipan and sliced almond pinecones are simple to make and, along with sprigs of rosemary and a dusting of confectioners' sugar, add a charming woodland touch.

½ recipe Marzipan (page 222)

FOR THE CAKE

⅓ cup (80 ml) canola oil, plus more for greasing

1⅔ cups (8½ oz/265 g) all-purpose flour, plus more for dusting

⅔ cup (2 oz/60 g) unsweetened cocoa powder

1 teaspoon baking powder

1 teaspoon baking soda

1 teaspoon kosher salt

1⅓ cups (11 oz/345 g) granulated sugar

2 large eggs

1 cup (250 ml) buttermilk

2 teaspoons pure vanilla extract

¼ lb (125 g) semisweet chocolate chips, melted and cooled

¾ teaspoon espresso powder

SERVES 12

Make the marzipan as directed and refrigerate; do not roll out the dough.

To make the cake, preheat the oven to 350°F (180°C). Grease a rimmed sheet cake pan, line the pan with parchment paper, then grease the parchment. Dust with flour, then tap out any excess.

In a bowl, sift together the flour, cocoa powder, baking powder, baking soda, and salt. Set aside.

In the bowl of a stand mixer fitted with the paddle attachment, beat together the granulated sugar, eggs, buttermilk, oil, and vanilla on medium speed until blended, about 2 minutes. Reduce the speed to low, slowly add the flour mixture, and beat until incorporated, stopping the mixer to scrape down the sides of the bowl as needed. Add the melted chocolate and espresso powder and beat until combined. Raise the speed to high and beat for 30 seconds.

Transfer the batter to the prepared cake pan and spread evenly. Bake until a toothpick inserted into the center of the cake comes out clean, about 20 minutes. Transfer the pan to a wire rack and let the cake cool for 15 minutes, then place a clean kitchen towel over the top of the cake. Invert the cake and towel onto a cutting board and peel off the parchment from the cake bottom. Starting at the short end of the cake, gently roll the cake away from you, rolling the towel as you go, until you form a log. Let cool until just barely warm, about 20 minutes.

Continued on next page

Continued from previous page

2 recipes Whipped Cream
(page 225)

1 recipe Chocolate Frosting
(page 223)

½ cup (2 oz/60 g) sliced almonds

4 fresh rosemary springs,
for garnish

Confectioners' sugar,
for dusting

Make the whipped cream and chocolate frosting.

Carefully unroll the cake and remove the kitchen towel. Spread the whipped cream evenly over the top of the cake, then reroll the cake. Using an offset spatula, spread the chocolate ganache frosting evenly over the rolled cake, then use the end of the spatula to create ridges and lines to look like tree bark.

To make the pinecones, using your hands, roll about ½ tablespoon of the marzipan dough into a ball. Starting at the bottom and working your way up, insert some of the almonds into the marzipan, creating a layered effect. Repeat with the remaining marzipan and almonds. The pinecones can be stored in an airtight container in the refrigerator for up to 1 day.

Decorate the cake with the pinecones and rosemary sprigs, dust with confectioners' sugar, and serve.

TIP *Roll the log slowly, using even pressure on both sides to prevent cracking. If the roll does crack, the whipped cream filling will hold the cake together. Refrigerate for 10 minutes before frosting with the ganache.*

Gingerbread Cake with Maple-Mascarpone Whipped Cream

Room-temperature cream cheese is imperative to achieving a cake with a silky-smooth texture. If you're pressed for time, unwrap the cheese and microwave it in 10-second bursts to bring it up to temperature.

FOR THE GINGERBREAD COOKIES

4 tablespoons (2 oz/60 g) unsalted butter, at room temperature

¼ cup (2 oz/60 g) firmly packed light brown sugar

3 tablespoons molasses

1 large egg yolk

1 cup (5 oz/155 g) all-purpose flour, plus more for dusting

¼ teaspoon baking soda

⅛ teaspoon kosher salt

1 teaspoon ground ginger

¼ teaspoon ground cinnamon

¼ teaspoon ground allspice

¼ teaspoon ground cloves

SERVES 12

To make the gingerbread cookies, in the bowl of a stand mixer fitted with the paddle attachment, beat together the butter and brown sugar on medium speed until light and fluffy, about 2 minutes. Add the molasses and egg yolk and beat until combined, stopping the mixer to scrape down the sides of the bowl as needed. Reduce the speed to low and add the flour, baking soda, salt, ginger, cinnamon, allspice, and cloves. Beat until combined, then raise the speed to medium and beat until a thick dough forms, about 1 minute. Turn the dough out onto a lightly floured work surface and shape into a disk. Wrap in plastic wrap and refrigerate for at least 1½ hours or up to 3 days.

Preheat the oven to 350°F (180°C). Line a baking sheet with parchment paper.

Let the dough stand at room temperature for about 20 minutes. On a lightly floured surface, roll out the dough ¼ inch (6 mm) thick. Using cookie cutters, cut out desired shapes, such as trees, snowmen, and gingerbread men, and transfer to the prepared baking sheet, spacing them about 2 inches (5 cm) apart. Bake until the edges of the cookies are set, 6–12 minutes, depending on their size. Transfer the cookies to wire racks and let cool completely.

Continued on next page

Continued from previous page

FOR THE CAKE

¾ cup (180 ml) canola oil, plus more for greasing

2 cups (10 oz/315 g) all-purpose flour, plus more for dusting

1 cup (250 ml) Guinness or oatmeal stout

¾ cup (8¼ oz/260 g) molasses

½ teaspoon baking soda

3 large eggs

1 teaspoon pure vanilla extract

1 cup (8 oz/250 g) granulated sugar

1 cup (7 oz/220 g) firmly packed light brown sugar

1½ teaspoons baking powder

1 teaspoon salt

3 tablespoons ground ginger

3 teaspoons ground cinnamon

½ teaspoon ground cloves

½ teaspoon ground nutmeg

¼ teaspoon ground cardamom

1 teaspoon maple extract

4 fresh rosemary sprigs

Confectioners' sugar, for dusting

FOR MASCARPONE WHIPPED CREAM

⅔ cup (5 oz/155 g) mascarpone cheese

1 cup (250 ml) heavy cream

¼ teaspoon pure vanilla extract

To make the cake, keep the oven set at 350°F (180°C). Grease three 8-inch (20-cm) round cake pans, line the bottoms of the pans with parchment paper, then grease the parchment. Dust with flour, then tap out any excess.

In a large saucepan over medium heat, combine the Guinness and molasses and bring to a boil. Remove from the heat and whisk in the baking soda. The mixture will bubble; continue to whisk until the bubbling subsides. Let cool completely.

In a large bowl, whisk together the eggs, vanilla, both sugars, and oil. Sift the flour, baking powder, salt, ginger, cinnamon, cloves, nutmeg, and cardamom over the egg mixture. Using a rubber spatula, fold until well combined into a cohesive batter. Add the Guinness mixture and stir until blended. The batter will be thin.

Divide the batter evenly among the prepared pans. Bake until a toothpick inserted into the center of the cakes comes out with just a few moist crumbs attached, 22–26 minutes. Transfer the pans to wire racks and let cool for 10 minutes, then invert the cakes onto the racks and let cool completely.

Make the mascarpone whipped cream, adding the maple extract along with the vanilla.

To assemble the cake, place 1 cake layer on a cake stand or serving plate. Spread one-third of the mascarpone whipped cream evenly over the cake. Repeat with the remaining cake layers, then spread the remaining whipped cream over the top of the cake. Gently stand the gingerbread cookies on top of the cake. Surround with the rosemary sprigs to resemble trees and dust the entire cake with confectioners' sugar to resemble snow. The cake can be stored in an airtight container in the refrigerator for up to 2 days.

MASCARPONE WHIPPED CREAM

In the bowl of a stand mixer fitted with the whisk attachment, beat together the mascarpone, cream, and vanilla on medium-high speed until stiff peaks form, about 3 minutes. Use right away, or cover and refrigerate for up to 2 hours.

VARIATION

To make Almond-Mascarpone Whipped Cream, add ½ teaspoon almond extract in place of the vanilla extract.

SNOWY COOKIES
Dust the remaining gingerbread cookies with confectioners' sugar.

MERRY & BRIGHT
This cake's flat top is the
ideal platform for an array
of festive candles.

Peppermint Devil's Food Cake

Chocolate and peppermint make great flavor partners and this tall masterpiece of a cake makes full use of them. Crushed candy canes serve two purposes: to add flavor and texture to the buttercream filling and to decorate the outside of the cake in a fun and festive way.

⅔ cup (5 oz/155 g) unsalted butter, at room temperature, plus more for greasing

1¾ cups (9 oz/280 g) all-purpose flour, plus more for dusting

1 cup (250 ml) hot brewed coffee

¾ cup (2¼ oz/65 g) unsweetened cocoa powder

1½ teaspoons baking soda

1 teaspoon kosher salt

2 cups (1 lb/500 g) sugar

3 large eggs

1½ teaspoons peppermint extract, plus 1 teaspoon for the vanilla buttercream

1 teaspoon pure vanilla extract

1¼ cups (310 ml) buttermilk

2 recipes Vanilla Buttercream (page 223)

1½ cups (4½ oz/135 g) crushed candy canes or peppermint candies

SERVES 12

Preheat the oven to 350°F (180°C). Grease two 8-inch (20-cm) round cake pans, line the bottoms of the pans with parchment paper, then grease the parchment. Dust with flour, then tap out any excess.

In a small bowl, whisk together the coffee and cocoa powder until no lumps remain. In a medium bowl, sift together the flour, baking soda, and salt. Set aside.

In the bowl of a stand mixer fitted with the paddle attachment, beat together the butter and sugar on medium speed until light and fluffy, about 2 minutes. Add the eggs one at a time, beating until incorporated after each addition, then add the peppermint and vanilla extracts and beat until combined, about 1 minute. Reduce the speed to low and add the flour mixture in 3 additions, alternating with the buttermilk, beginning and ending with the flour. Beat in the last addition just until the flour disappears, about 30 seconds. Add the coffee mixture and beat until uniformly combined.

Divide the batter evenly between the prepared pans and spread evenly. Bake until a toothpick inserted into the center of the cakes comes out clean, about 40 minutes. Transfer the pans to wire racks and let cool for 10 minutes, then invert the cakes onto the racks and let cool completely.

Make the vanilla buttercream; for each batch, replace ½ teaspoon of the vanilla extract with ½ teaspoon peppermint extract. Stir ¾ cup (2¼ oz/68 g) of the crushed candy canes into 1 batch.

To assemble the cake, using a large serrated knife, cut each cake in half horizontally to create 4 thin layers. Place the bottom layer on a cake stand or serving plate. Spread one-third of the candy cane buttercream evenly over the cake. Repeat with the remaining cake layers. Cover the entire cake with a crumb coat of peppermint buttercream and refrigerate for 30 minutes. Spread the remaining peppermint buttercream over the top and sides of the chilled cake. Press the remaining ¾ cup (2¼ oz/68 g) crushed candy canes against the sides and serve.

TIP *To crush the candy canes or the peppermint candies, seal the candy in a lock-top plastic bag and crush with a frying pan or rolling pin to the desired texture.*

Classic Cheesecake

Room-temperature cream cheese is imperative to achieving a cheesecake with a silky-smooth texture. Using cold cream cheese creates a lumpy cheesecake.

FOR THE CRUST

7 oz (220 g) graham crackers, about 11 graham crackers

¼ cup (1¾ oz/50 g) sugar

6 tablespoons (3 oz/90 g) unsalted butter, melted and cooled

Pinch of kosher salt

FOR THE FILLING

1½ lb (680 g) cream cheese, at room temperature

¾ cup (5 oz/140 g) plus 2 tablespoons sugar

½ teaspoon kosher salt

¾ cup (6 oz/170 g) sour cream, at room temperature

2½ teaspoons vanilla bean paste

3 large eggs, at room temperature

1 tablespoon fresh lemon juice

Whipped Cream (page 225), for serving

SERVES 10

To make the crust, preheat the oven to 350°F (180°C). Tightly wrap the bottom half of a 9-inch (23-cm) springform pan with aluminum foil.

In a food processor, pulse the graham crackers until fine crumbs form. Transfer to a bowl. Add the sugar, melted butter, and salt and stir until a cohesive mixture forms that resembles wet sand. Using the bottom of a measuring cup, press the crumb mixture firmly into the bottom and 1 inch (2.5 cm) up the sides of the prepared pan.

Bake until the crust is golden, 12–15 minutes. Transfer the pan to a wire rack and let cool completely. Reduce the oven temperature to 325°F (165°C).

Meanwhile, make the filling: In the bowl of a stand mixer fitted with the paddle attachment, beat the cream cheese on medium-high speed until smooth, about 3 minutes. Add the sugar, salt, sour cream, and vanilla and beat until combined, about 2 minutes, stopping the mixer to scrape down the sides of the bowl as needed. Add the eggs one at a time and beat on low speed until just combined, then add lemon juice and raise the speed to medium-high and beat until smooth, about 1 minute.

Transfer the filling to the cooled crust and spread evenly. Place the springform pan in a large roasting pan or ovenproof saucepan. Pour water into the roasting pan to reach 1 inch (2.5 cm) up the sides of the springform pan.

Bake until the edges of the cheesecake are set but the center still jiggles when gently shaken, about 1 hour and 10 minutes.

Transfer the springform pan to a wire rack and let cool completely. Cover with aluminum foil and refrigerate until the cheesecake is firm, at least 2 hours or up to overnight. To serve, remove the outer ring of the pan. Cut the cheesecake into wedges and serve with whipped cream.

Continued on page 116

Continued from page 114

FOR THE STRAWBERRY TOPPING

1 lb (about ½ kg) strawberries

1 tbsp lemon juice

3 tbsp sugar

FOR THE LEMON CURD

2 teaspoons grated lemon zest

½ cup (120 ml) fresh lemon juice

¾ cup (5 oz/140 g) sugar

3 large eggs

4 tablespoons (2 oz/60 g) unsalted butter, cut into small pieces

VARIATIONS

Cheesecake with Strawberries

In a bowl, stir together the strawberries, lemon juice, and sugar. Let sit for at least 5 minutes, until the strawberries begin to release some juices. Use as a topping or serve with whipped cream.

Lemon Cheesecake

In a saucepan over medium-low heat, whisk together lemon zest, lemon juice, sugar, and 3 eggs. Add the butter in 3 additions, whisking constantly until fully melted before adding more. Cook, whisking constantly, until the mixture is thick enough to coat the back of a spoon, about 5 minutes. Strain the curd through a fine-mesh sieve into a bowl. Press plastic wrap directly onto the surface of the curd and refrigerate until chilled, at least 30 minutes or up to 3 days. Make the crust as directed. When transferring the filling to the cooled crust, dollop the chilled lemon curd over the filling, then use a toothpick or skewer to swirl the curd into the filling, taking care not to overmix. Bake as directed for 1 hour and 15 minutes.

Bourbon Pumpkin Cheesecake

Here, rich pumpkin cheesecake gets a lift from sweet bourbon and plenty of warm spices. This cheesecake would be a welcome finale to a festive holiday meal. Bonus! You can make the cheesecake a day in advance—in fact, it's even better the next day.

FOR THE CRUST

7 oz (220 g) graham crackers

2 tablespoons firmly packed light brown sugar

⅔ cup (5 oz/155 g) unsalted butter, melted and cooled

Pinch of kosher salt

FOR THE FILLING

1 can (15 oz/470 g) pumpkin purée

2 large eggs plus 2 large egg yolks

½ cup (3½ oz/105 g) firmly packed light brown sugar

⅓ cup (80 ml) bourbon

3 tablespoons heavy cream

2 tablespoons fresh lemon juice

1 vanilla bean, split and seeds scraped, seeds reserved

1 tablespoon cornstarch

½ teaspoon kosher salt

2 teaspoons ground cinnamon

1 teaspoon each ground ginger and nutmeg

1½ lb (750 g) cream cheese, at room temperature

Whipped Cream (page 225), for serving

SERVES 12

To make the graham cracker crust, in a food processor, pulse the graham crackers until the texture resembles sand. Add the brown sugar, melted butter, and salt and pulse until the texture resembles wet sand. Gently press the crust mixture evenly into the bottom and up the sides of a 9-inch (23-cm) springform pan. Refrigerate for 1 hour.

Preheat the oven to 350°F (180°C). To make the filling, in a bowl, whisk together the pumpkin purée, eggs, egg yolks, brown sugar, bourbon, cream, lemon juice, and vanilla bean seeds. Set aside.

In the bowl of a stand mixer, using a handheld whisk, whisk together the cornstarch, salt, cinnamon, ginger, and nutmeg. Add the cream cheese, then attach the bowl to the mixer fitted with the paddle attachment and beat on medium-high speed until smooth, about 3 minutes. Stop the mixer and scrape down the sides of the bowl. Add the pumpkin mixture and beat on low speed until blended, about 3 minutes.

Pour the filling into the chilled crust and place the pan on a baking sheet. Bake until the center is just set, 50–60 minutes. Transfer the pan to a wire rack and let cool to room temperature, then refrigerate until firm, at least 4 hours and preferably overnight. Remove the outer ring of the pan.

Just before serving, make the whipped cream and spread it over the chilled cheesecake, then serve.

PIES & TARTS

Salted Caramel Apple Pie

There is no pie that is more classic than an apple pie. Our favorite baking apples are Gala, but Granny Smith or Pink Lady apples also make a great pie. Look for baking apples with a sweet-tart flavor that hold their shape and don't turn to mush.

2 recipes Basic Pie Dough (page 213), rolled into 2 rounds

1½ cups (12 oz/375 g) granulated sugar

1 tablespoon, plus 1 teaspoon fresh lemon juice

1½ cups (375 ml) heavy cream

2 teaspoons sea salt

5 lb (2½ kg) Granny Smith apples, peeled, cored, and each apple cut into 8 slices

½ cup (3½ oz/105 g) firmly packed light brown sugar

½ teaspoon cinnamon

¼ teaspoon ground nutmeg

3 tablespoons cornstarch

1 large egg beaten with 1 teaspoon water

Turbinado sugar, for sprinkling

Flake sea salt, for sprinkling

SERVES 8-10

Make the pie dough. Fit 1 dough round into a 9-inch (23-cm) deep-dish pie dish and trim the edges flush with the rim. Refrigerate for 30 minutes.

In a large saucepan over medium heat, combine the granulated sugar, ¼ cup (60 ml) water, and the 1 teaspoon lemon juice. Cook until the mixture bubbles vigorously and turns a golden amber color, about 9 minutes. Remove from the heat and carefully add the cream, stirring until the sauce is blended. Stir in 1½ teaspoons of the salt and let cool until just warm.

Meanwhile, preheat the oven to 350°F (180°C).

In a large pot over medium heat, stir together the apples, brown sugar, cinnamon, nutmeg, and the 1 tablespoon lemon juice. Cover and cook, stirring occasionally, until the apples are just tender, 10–12 minutes. Uncover and let cool to room temperature. Stir in the cornstarch, the remaining ½ teaspoon salt, and ¾ cup (180 ml) of the sauce to the apple mixture and stir together; reserve the remaining sauce for serving.

Pour the filling into the crust. Place the remaining dough round over the filling, trim the edges flush with the rim, and press the top and bottom crusts together. Brush the crust with the egg mixture and sprinkle with turbinado sugar. Place the pie dish on a baking sheet.

Bake until the crust is golden brown and the filling is bubbling, about 1 hour, covering the top and edges with aluminum foil if they brown too quickly. Let cool on a wire rack for at least 4 hours, preferably overnight, before serving.

Reheat the reserved sauce over low heat until just warm. Sprinkle the pie with flake salt, slice, and serve with the sauce.

TIP *To save time, use store-bought caramel sauce instead of the homemade version here.*

Maple-Pecan Pie
with Shortbread Crust

For many, it just isn't autumn without a toasty pecan pie. The dark sweetness of maple brings out the pecan flavor, and a toothsome shortbread crust is a nice contrast to the texture of this striking pie.

1 recipe Shortbread Crust (page 214), baked and cooled

1½ cups (16½ oz/465 g) pure maple syrup

3 large eggs, lightly beaten

¼ cup (2 oz/60 g) granulated sugar

¼ cup (2 oz/60 g) firmly packed dark brown sugar

¼ teaspoon kosher salt

4 tablespoons (2 oz/60 g) unsalted butter, melted and cooled

1 teaspoon pure vanilla extract

3 tablespoons all-purpose flour

2 tablespoons heavy cream

2 cups (8 oz/250 g) pecans, toasted and chopped

SERVES 8-10

Make the shortbread crust.

Preheat the oven to 350°F (180°C).

In a saucepan over medium-high heat, bring the maple syrup to a boil and boil until reduced to 1 cup (11 oz/310 g), 8–10 minutes. Let cool to room temperature.

In a large bowl, stir together the eggs, granulated sugar, brown sugar, reduced maple syrup, salt, melted butter, and vanilla until smooth and blended. Stir in the flour and cream and then the pecans. Pour the filling into the crust.

Bake until the center is slightly puffed and firm to the touch, 30–40 minutes, covering the edges with aluminum foil if they brown too quickly. Let cool on a wire rack until just slightly warm, about 45 minutes, before serving.

TIP *For a pretty visual effect, keep the pecans whole and arrange on top of the unbaked pie instead of stirring them into the filling.*

Cranberry Pie

This jewel-toned lattice-topped pie is a great way to finish a hearty feast. For the holidays, instead of a lattice-topped pie, use a holiday-themed cookie cutter to cut out pieces of rolled-out pie dough and then layer them over the top in a pretty pattern.

2 recipes Basic Pie Dough (page 213), rolled into 2 rounds

9 cups (2¼ lb/1.1 kg) fresh or thawed frozen cranberries

2¼ cups (1 lb/500 g) firmly packed light brown sugar

¼ cup (1 oz/30 g) plus 1 tablespoon cornstarch

1½ tablespoons grated orange zest

½ cup (125 ml) fresh orange juice

1 teaspoon cinnamon

¼ teaspoon ground nutmeg

¼ teaspoon ground cloves

1 teaspoon pure vanilla extract

1 large egg beaten with 1 teaspoon water

Turbinado sugar, for sprinkling

SERVES 10

Make the pie dough. Fit 1 dough round into a 9-inch (23-cm) deep-dish pie dish and trim the edges flush with the rim. Refrigerate for 30 minutes.

Meanwhile, preheat the oven to 350°F (180°C).

In a large saucepan over medium heat, combine the cranberries, brown sugar, cornstarch, orange zest and juice, cinnamon, nutmeg, and cloves. Cook, stirring occasionally, until the cranberries soften and release their juice, 8–10 minutes. Stir in the vanilla and let cool to room temperature.

Pour the filling into the crust. Using the remaining dough round, create a modern lattice pattern (see page 234). Brush the crust with the egg mixture and sprinkle with turbinado sugar. Place the pie dish on a baking sheet.

Bake until the crust is golden brown and the filling is bubbling, about 1 hour, covering the top and edges with aluminum foil if they brown too quickly. Let cool on a wire rack for at least 4 hours, preferably overnight, before serving.

Blueberry-Cardamom Pie

Cardamom adds a warm, exotic note to this otherwise classic pie. Be sure to use the full amount of thickener, as blueberries can be very juicy, especially when they are fresh and sweet in early summer.

2 recipes Basic Pie Dough (page 213)

4 pints (2 lb/1 kg) fresh or thawed frozen blueberries

1¼ cups (10 oz/315 g) granulated sugar

1 teaspoon grated lemon zest

2 tablespoons fresh lemon juice

½ teaspoon ground cardamom

Pinch of kosher salt

¼ cup (1 oz/30 g) cornstarch

2 tablespoons unsalted butter, diced

1 large egg beaten with 1 teaspoon water

Turbinado sugar, for sprinkling

SERVES 8-10

Make the pie dough. Roll 1 dough into a round and fit into a 9-inch (23-cm) deep-dish pie dish and trim the overhang to ½ inch (12 mm), fold the edge under itself, and decoratively flute. Refrigerate the pie shell and the remaining dough for 30 minutes.

Meanwhile, preheat the oven to 350°F (180°C).

In a large saucepan over medium heat, combine the blueberries, granulated sugar, lemon zest and juice, cardamom, and salt. Cook, stirring occasionally, until some of the berries begin to burst and the liquid reduces slightly, 5–7 minutes. Remove from the heat and fold in the cornstarch. Let cool to room temperature.

Transfer the remaining dough to a work surface and roll out into a long rectangle, about 6-by-18-inches (15-by-45-cm). Cut the rectangle lengthwise into six 1-inch (2.5-cm) wide strips. Remove the pie shell from the refrigerator, pour in the filling, and dot with the butter. Carefully twist 1 strip of dough. Starting at the center of the pie, gently lay the twisted strip of dough in a circular pattern. Pinch the end of a second strip to the first to seal, then twist and coil the second strip around the first. Continue to add the remaining dough strips, circling them over the pie filling. Brush the crust with the egg mixture and sprinkle with turbinado sugar. Place the pie dish on a baking sheet.

Bake until the crust is golden brown and the filling is bubbling, 50–55 minutes, covering the top and edges with aluminum foil if they brown too quickly. Let cool on a wire rack for at least 4 hours, preferably overnight, before serving.

TIP *Try other types of berries, such as blackberries or strawberries or a combination.*

Strawberry-Rhubarb Crumble Pie

Sweet springtime fruits shine in this delicious pie topped with crunchy oat-based streusel. Whether you use a strawberry-rhubarb combination, all berries, or all rhubarb, you are certain to bring smiles to everyone's faces when you serve this pie.

1 recipe Basic Pie Dough (page 213), rolled into 1 round

FOR THE OAT CRUMBLE TOPPING

⅓ cup (2 oz/60 g) all-purpose flour

⅓ cup (1 oz/30 g) rolled oats

⅓ cup (2½ oz/75 g) firmly packed light brown sugar

½ teaspoon ground ginger

¼ teaspoon kosher salt

1 teaspoon grated orange zest

½ cup (4 oz/125 g) unsalted butter, melted and cooled)

FOR THE FILLING

1 cup (8 oz/250 g) sugar

⅓ cup (1½ oz/45 g) cornstarch

1 teaspoon kosher salt

3 pints (1½ lb/750 g) strawberries, stemmed, cored, and thickly sliced

1½ lb (750 g) rhubarb, trimmed and cut into ¾-inch (2-cm) pieces

1 teaspoon grated orange zest

2 teaspoons fresh orange juice

Vanilla ice cream, for serving

SERVES 8-10

Make the pie dough. Fit the dough round into a 9-inch (23-cm) pie dish. Trim the overhang to ½ inch (12 mm), fold the edge under itself, and decoratively flute or crimp. Pierce the bottom of the crust all over with a fork and freeze for 30 minutes.

Make the crumble topping: In a medium bowl, whisk together the flour, oats, brown sugar, ginger, salt, and orange zest. Stir in the melted butter. Refrigerate until ready to use.

Preheat the oven to 375°F (190°C).

In a large bowl, whisk together the sugar, cornstarch, and salt. Add the strawberries and rhubarb and stir to combine. Let stand for 20 minutes, then drain off the excess liquid. Stir in the orange zest and juice. Pour the filling into the crust. Sprinkle with the crumble topping and place the pie dish on a baking sheet.

Bake until the crust is golden brown and the filling is bubbling, 45–55 minutes, covering the top and edges with aluminum foil if they brown too quickly. Let cool on a wire rack for at least 4 hours, preferably overnight, before serving. Serve with vanilla ice cream.

TIP *If you can't find rhubarb, make an all-strawberry pie or substitute another fresh berry to total 3 lb (1.5 kg) of fruit.*

Peach Pie

A bountiful, juicy peach pie is the epitome of summertime. This sunny dessert is best made when peaches are at their ripe, fragrant best late in the season. We love the simplicity of this pie with just a scoop of vanilla ice cream.

2 recipes Basic Pie Dough (page XX), rolled into 2 rounds

2 lb (1 kg) peaches, peeled, pitted, and sliced

1 tablespoon fresh lemon juice

⅓ cup (3 oz/90 g) granulated sugar

2 tablespoons cornstarch

¼ teaspoon kosher salt

Pinch of cinnamon

1 large egg beaten with 1 teaspoon water

Turbinado sugar, for sprinkling

SERVES 8-10

Make the pie dough. Fit 1 dough round into a 9-inch (23-cm) deep-dish pie dish and trim the edges flush with the rim. Refrigerate the pie shell and the remaining dough round for 30 minutes.

Meanwhile, preheat the oven to 350°F (180°C).

In a large bowl, toss together the peaches and lemon juice. In a small bowl, stir together the granulated sugar, cornstarch, salt, and cinnamon. Add to the peaches and toss to combine. Pour the filling into the crust.

Transfer the remaining dough round to a work surface and cut into lattice strips. Arrange the dough strips in a classic lattice form (see page 234). Brush the crust with the egg mixture and sprinkle with turbinado sugar. Place the pie dish on a baking sheet.

Bake until the crust is golden brown and the filling is bubbling, 45–50 minutes, covering the top and edges with aluminum foil if they brown too quickly. Let cool on a wire rack for at least 4 hours, preferably overnight, before serving.

TIP *In place of peaches, try fresh nectarines. Frozen peaches also work well; be sure to thaw them and drain off the liquid.*

Cherry Slab Pie

If you are feeding a crowd, there's nothing better than a slab pie, which can be made in a deep rimmed baking sheet. Because the pie doesn't have a base, it's easy to serve up big scoops. Try this with other summer fruits at your next barbecue.

2 recipes Basic Pie Dough (page 213), rolled into 2 rounds

14 cups pitted fresh or thawed frozen cherries (about 4½ lb/2.25 kg)

¾–1 cup (6–8 oz/185–245 g) granulated sugar (depending on the tartness of the cherries)

3 tablespoons cornstarch

1½ tablespoons almond meal

2 teaspoons grated lemon zest

1½ teaspoons almond extract

Pinch of kosher salt

1 large egg beaten with 1 teaspoon water

Turbinado sugar, for sprinkling

SERVES 10-12

Make the pie dough. Preheat the oven to 350°F (180°C).

In a large bowl, toss together the cherries, ¾ cup (6 oz/185 g) of the granulated sugar, the cornstarch, almond meal, lemon zest, almond extract, and salt. Taste and add up to ¼ cup (2 oz/60 g) more sugar, if desired. Transfer the filling to a rimmed half sheet pan and spread evenly.

Using a 3-inch (7.5-cm) round cutter, cut out enough rounds to cover the pie, gathering the scraps of dough and rerolling as needed. Place the rounds over the pie filling, overlapping slightly. Brush the crust with the egg mixture and sprinkle with turbinado sugar.

Bake until the crust is golden brown and the filling is bubbling, about 45 minutes, covering the top with aluminum foil if it browns too quickly. Let cool on a wire rack for at least 4 hours, preferably overnight, before serving.

Chocolate Checkerboard Raspberry Pie

This lattice pie uses two kinds of pie dough, chocolate and plain, for a gorgeous effect! The woven lattice hides a sweet filling of fresh raspberries spiked with Chambord. This is a great pie for your next party.

2 recipes Chocolate Pie Dough (page 214), rolled into 2 rounds

1 recipe Basic Pie Dough (page 213), rolled into 1 round

5 pints (2½ lb/1.25 kg) fresh or thawed frozen raspberries

¼ cup (1 oz/30 g) cornstarch

1 cup (8 oz/250 g) granulated sugar

2 tablespoons Chambord raspberry liqueur

Zest of 1 lemon

Pinch of kosher salt

1 large egg beaten with 1 teaspoon water

Turbinado sugar, for sprinkling

SERVES 6-8

Make the pie doughs. Fit a chocolate dough round into a 9-inch (23-cm) pie dish. Trim the overhang to ½ inch (12 mm), fold the edge under itself, and decoratively crimp. Refrigerate the pie shell and the remaining 2 dough rounds for 30 minutes.

Meanwhile, preheat the oven to 350°F (180°C).

Transfer the remaining chocolate dough round to a work surface and cut out 2-inch (5-cm) lattice strips. Repeat with the basic pie dough round. Refrigerate until ready to use.

In a large bowl, stir together the raspberries, cornstarch, granulated sugar, liqueur, lemon zest, and salt. Pour the filling into the crust.

Create a checkerboard lattice on top by laying all of the chocolate strips close together with a small gap between them on top of the filling. Weave the basic pie dough strips in a classic lattice pattern with the chocolate strips (see page 234). Trim off any excess dough. Brush the crust with the egg mixture and sprinkle with turbinado sugar. Place the pie dish on a baking sheet.

Bake until the crust is golden brown and the filling is bubbling, about 1 hour, covering the top and edges with aluminum foil if they brown too quickly. Let cool on a wire rack for at least 4 hours, preferably overnight, before serving.

Apple Hand Pies

Perfect for a picnic, these adorable little pies have the added surprise of pistachios, which you can leave out if you like, but we don't recommend it. You can make these in all different shapes: rounds as instructed, squares, or folded over into triangles or half circles.

2 recipes Basic Pie Dough (page 213), rolled into 2 rounds

¼ cup (2 oz/60 g) granulated sugar

2 lb (1 kg) Pink Lady or Fuji apples, peeled, cored, and cut into ⅛-inch (3-mm) slices

1 teaspoon cinnamon

¼ teaspoon ground cardamom

¼ teaspoon kosher salt

½ cup (2 oz/60 g) unsalted pistachios, toasted and chopped

Zest and juice of 1 lemon

1 large egg beaten with 1 teaspoon water

Turbinado sugar, for sprinkling

Vanilla ice cream, for serving

MAKES 10 HAND PIES

Make the pie dough. Using a 4-inch (10-cm) round cutter, cut out 20 rounds, gathering the scraps of dough and rerolling as needed. Cover with plastic wrap and refrigerate until ready to use. Let stand at room temperature for about 10 minutes before assembling the pies.

In a large sauté pan over medium heat, combine the granulated sugar and ¾ cup (180 ml) water and cook, stirring, until the sugar is dissolved. Add the apples, cinnamon, cardamom, and salt. Cook, stirring occasionally, until the apples are just tender and the liquid is slightly thickened, 6–8 minutes. Transfer to a bowl and stir in the pistachios and lemon zest and juice. Let cool to room temperature.

Meanwhile, preheat the oven to 400°F (200°C). Line a baking sheet with parchment paper.

Space half of the dough rounds on the prepared baking sheet, at least 1 inch (2.5 cm) apart. Brush them with some of the egg mixture, then place about ¼ cup (1 oz/30 g) of the apple filling in the center of each. Top each with a remaining dough round. Press the top and bottom edges together, then crimp with a fork. Brush the tops with the egg mixture and cut small steam vents. Sprinkle with turbinado sugar.

Bake until the crust is golden brown, 18–22 minutes. Let cool for 5 minutes. Serve warm or at room temperature with a scoop of vanilla ice cream.

TIP *Mini tart pans also work great in this recipe. Line each well with a pie dough round, then fill, top with another round, and bake as directed.*

Banana Cream Pie

The addition of rum and spices takes this special pie over the top. We use vanilla bean for both the flavor and the pretty seeds that show up in the custard, but you can substitute 1 teaspoon pure vanilla extract if you like.

1 recipe vanilla cookie Wafer Cookie Crust (page 215), baked and cooled

4 bananas

6 tablespoons (3 oz/90 g) unsalted butter

¼ cup (2 oz/60 g) firmly packed light brown sugar

½ teaspoon ground allspice

½ teaspoon ground nutmeg

¼ cup (60 ml) rum

3 cups (750 ml) whole milk

⅓ cup (1½ oz/45 g) cornstarch

4 large egg yolks

⅔ cup (5 oz/155 g) granulated sugar

⅛ teaspoon kosher salt

1 vanilla bean, split and seeds scraped, seeds and pod reserved

1 recipe Whipped Cream (page 225)

1 recipe Caramel Sauce (page 120)

SERVES 8-10

Make the wafer cookie crust.

Halve crosswise 2 of the bananas, then cut into thin slices. In a large sauté pan over medium heat, combine 4 tablespoons (2 oz/60 g) of the butter, the brown sugar, allspice, and nutmeg and stir until the sugar is dissolved, about 2 minutes. Add the banana slices and gently stir until the liquid thickens slightly and the bananas are coated, 3–4 minutes. Remove the pan from the heat, add the rum, then place over medium-high heat, and simmer until the liquid reduces to a syrup glaze, 4–6 minutes. Let cool to room temperature. Spread the mixture in the crust. Thinly slice the remaining 2 bananas and arrange on top.

In a small bowl, whisk together ½ cup (125 ml) of the milk and the cornstarch. In a large bowl, whisk the egg yolks until blended, then slowly whisk in the milk mixture. In a large saucepan over medium heat, combine the remaining 2½ cups (625 ml) milk, the granulated sugar, salt, and vanilla bean seeds and pod and bring to a simmer, stirring to dissolve the sugar. Remove from the heat and let stand for 5 minutes. Discard the vanilla pod.

Add the hot milk, ¼ cup (60 ml) at a time, to the egg mixture, whisking constantly, then pour the mixture back into the pan. Stir constantly over medium-high heat until the mixture boils. Reduce the heat to medium and stir constantly until the mixture is thick enough to coat the spoon, 6–8 minutes. Pour through a fine-mesh sieve into a large bowl. Stir in the remaining 2 tablespoons butter until melted. Press plastic wrap directly onto the surface and pierce the plastic a few times with a knife to let the steam escape. Let cool to room temperature. Spread the custard on top of the bananas.

Make the whipped cream. Pipe or spoon over the pie. Drizzle the caramel sauce over the cream. Refrigerate for at least 2 hours or up to overnight before serving.

TIP *You can replace the homemade caramel sauce with your favorite jarred caramel sauce from the store.*

Meyer Lemon Chess Pie

Chess pie, a simple yet flavorful custard pie that is a mainstay of the South, is freshened up with the addition of fragrant Meyer lemons. If you don't have access to Meyer lemons, by all means use more readily available Eureka lemons.

1 recipe Basic Pie Dough (page 213), rolled into 1 round

3 tablespoons all-purpose flour

3 tablespoons finely ground cornmeal

1 cup (8 oz/250 g) sugar

1 teaspoon pure vanilla extract

⅓ cup (2½ oz/75 g) crème fraîche

4 large eggs, lightly beaten

1 cup (250 ml) buttermilk

6 tablespoons (3 oz/90 g) unsalted butter, melted and cooled slightly

Zest of 2 Meyer lemons

Raspberries, for serving (optional)

Confectioners' sugar, for dusting (optional)

SERVES 8-10

Make the pie dough. Fit the dough round into a 9-inch (23-cm) deep-dish pie dish. Trim the overhang to ½ inch (12 mm), fold the edge under itself, and decoratively flute or crimp. Freeze for 30 minutes.

Meanwhile, preheat the oven to 350°F (180°C).

Line the crust with aluminum foil and fill with pie weights. Bake until lightly browned and dry to the touch, about 20 minutes. Remove the foil and weights, and set on a wire rack to cool completely. Keep the oven set.

In a large bowl, stir together the flour, cornmeal, sugar, vanilla, crème fraîche, eggs, and buttermilk. Fold in the melted butter and lemon zest. Pour the filling into the crust.

Bake until slightly puffed and golden brown, 45–50 minutes, covering the top and edges with aluminum foil if they brown too quickly. Let cool completely on a wire rack. Decorate with raspberries and dust with confectioners' sugar, if using, before serving.

Toasted-Coconut Cream Pie

Seek out good-quality shredded and flaked coconut for this fragrant and creamy pie, and be sure to choose unsweetened. Toast the flaked coconut by spreading it on a baking sheet and toasting in a 325°F (165°C) oven, stirring once or twice, for about 5 minutes.

1 recipe vanilla cookie Wafer Cookie Crust (page 215), baked and cooled

1½ cups (375 ml) whole milk

1½ cups (375 ml) coconut milk

3 large eggs plus 2 large egg yolks

¾ cup (6 oz/185 g) sugar

¼ cup (1½ oz/45 g) all-purpose flour

¼ teaspoon kosher salt

1½ teaspoons pure vanilla extract

1 cup (4 oz/125 g) shredded dried unsweetened coconut (optional)

1 recipe Whipped Cream (page 225)

½ cup (1½ oz/45 g) toasted flaked unsweetened coconut

SERVES 8-10

Make the wafer cookie crust.

In a saucepan over medium heat, combine the milk and coconut milk and warm until it just begins to simmer.

In a large bowl, whisk together the eggs, egg yolks, sugar, flour, and salt until smooth. Add the hot milk mixture, ¼ cup (60 ml) at a time, to the egg mixture, whisking constantly, then pour the mixture back into the pan. Cook, stirring constantly over medium-high heat until the mixture boils. Reduce the heat to medium and stir constantly until the mixture is thick enough to coat the spoon, 6–8 minutes.

Pour the mixture through a fine-mesh sieve into a large bowl. Stir in the vanilla and shredded coconut (if using). Let cool to room temperature. Pour the filling into the crust.

Make the topping. Pipe or spoon the whipped cream over the pie and garnish with the flaked coconut. Refrigerate for at least 2 hours or up to overnight before serving.

Dulce de Leche Ice Cream Pie

The great thing about this modern ice cream pie, besides its creamy decadence, is that it can be made up to a week ahead! Which means you can make it anytime and serve it at a moment's notice.

1 recipe vanilla cookie Wafer Cookie Crust (page 215), baked and cooled

1 cup (7 oz/220 g) firmly packed light brown sugar

½ cup (125 ml) half-and-half

4 tablespoons (2 oz/60 g) unsalted butter

1 teaspoon kosher salt

1 tablespoon pure vanilla extract

2 pints (1¾ lb/880 g) dulce de leche ice cream, softened

1⅔ cups (6½ oz/200 g) pecans, toasted and chopped

SERVES 8–10

Make the wafer cookie crust.

In a small saucepan over medium-low heat, combine the brown sugar, half-and-half, butter, and salt. Cook, whisking gently, until the sauce thickens, 5–7 minutes. Stir in the vanilla and cook for 1 minute longer. Transfer the caramel sauce to a small bowl and let cool to room temperature.

Spread 1 pint (14 oz/440 g) of the ice cream evenly over the crust. Freeze until almost firm, about 1 hour. Reserve ¼ cup (60 ml) of the caramel sauce for drizzling and spread the rest evenly over the ice cream. Layer the pecans on top, reserving ¼ cup (1 oz/30 g) of the pecans for garnish, if desired. Freeze until the caramel hardens, about 20 minutes. Spread the remaining 1 pint (14 oz/440 g) ice cream evenly over the caramel-pecan layer. Freeze until firm, about 1 hour.

Drizzle the reserved caramel sauce over the pie. Sprinkle the reserved pecans, if using, around the edges. Freeze until ready to serve, up to 1 week.

TIP *To soften the ice cream, place it in the refrigerator for 1–2 hours before using.*

You can also make this recipe with a graham cracker crust (page 114) for a classic key lime pie.

Key Lime Pie with Pretzel Crust

Similar to a graham cracker crust, this salty-sweet pretzel shell pairs beautifully with the zesty, fragrant key lime filling. Look for bottled key lime juice, or, if you are lucky enough to find them, use fresh key limes.

1 recipe Pretzel Crust (page 215), baked and cooled

8 large egg yolks

2 cans (14 fl oz/430 ml each) sweetened condensed milk

4 teaspoons grated lime zest

1 cup (250 ml) key lime juice

1 recipe Whipped Cream (page 225)

Grated lime zest, for garnish (optional)

Turbinado sugar, for sprinkling (optional)

SERVES 8-10

Make the pretzel crust. Preheat the oven to 350°F (180°C).

In a large bowl, whisk together the egg yolks until well blended. Add the condensed milk and lime zest and juice and whisk to combine. Pour the filling into the crust. Place the pie dish on a baking sheet.

Bake until the edges of the pie are set but the center still jiggles slightly, 18–22 minutes. Let cool completely on a wire rack. Refrigerate for at least 2 hours or up to overnight before serving.

Make the topping. Pipe or spoon the whipped cream over the cooled pie. Garnish with lime zest and sprinkle with turbinado sugar, if using.

TIP *Pour in the filling until it just reaches the top of the pretzel crust; you may have some left over depending on the size of your pie dish.*

Butterscotch-Bourbon Pie

Dark brown sugar, brown butter, and bourbon give this butterscotch pie deep flavor. To cut the density, we like to serve it with lightly whipped cream. Be sure to choose a sweet bourbon that you'd enjoy serving alongside.

1 recipe Basic Pie Dough (page 213), rolled into 1 round

1½ cups (375 ml) whole milk

1½ cups (375 ml) heavy cream

1 vanilla bean, split and seeds scraped, seeds and pod reserved

4 tablespoons (2 oz/60 g) unsalted butter

¾ cup (6 oz/185 g) firmly packed dark brown sugar

9 large egg yolks

3 tablespoons cornstarch

1 teaspoon kosher salt

2 tablespoons bourbon

1 teaspoon fresh lemon juice

1 recipe Whipped Cream (page 225), for serving

SERVES 8-10

Make the pie dough. Fit the dough round into a 9-inch (23-cm) pie dish. Trim the overhang to ½ inch (12 mm), fold the edge under itself, and decoratively flute or crimp. Pierce the bottom of the crust all over with a fork and freeze for 30 minutes.

Meanwhile, preheat the oven to 350°F (180°C). Line the crust with aluminum foil and fill with pie weights. Bake until lightly browned, about 15 minutes. Remove the foil and weights and cook completely, 10–15 minutes longer. Set on a wire rack to cool completely. Keep the oven set.

In a small saucepan over medium heat, combine the milk, cream, and vanilla bean seeds and pod and bring to a gentle simmer. Remove from the heat and let stand for 5 minutes. Discard the vanilla pod.

In a large saucepan over medium heat, melt the butter. Reduce the heat to low and cook until the milk solids are golden with a nutty fragrance, but not burned, about 6 minutes. Stir in half of the brown sugar and the milk mixture. Remove from the heat.

In a large bowl, whisk together the egg yolks, cornstarch, salt, and the remaining brown sugar until well blended. Add the hot milk, ¼ cup (60 ml) at a time, to the egg mixture, whisking constantly, then pour the mixture back into the pan. Stir constantly over medium-high heat until the mixture boils. Reduce the heat to medium and stir constantly until the mixture is thick enough to coat the spoon, 6–8 minutes. Pour the mixture through a fine-mesh sieve into a large bowl. Stir in the bourbon and lemon juice. Pour the filling into the crust.

Bake until the edges are set but the center jiggles slightly, 25–35 minutes, covering the edges with aluminum foil if they brown too quickly. Let cool completely on a wire rack. Serve at room temperature or chilled for at least 2 hours or up to overnight. Top with whipped cream and serve.

TIP *No vanilla bean? No problem! Use 1 teaspoon pure vanilla extract instead, in the same way you use the vanilla bean.*

Salty Honey Pie

If you've never had or heard of salty honey pie, you are in for a treat! This custard-filled pie is similar to a chess pie or buttermilk pie, but with plenty of honey-toned flavor. For contrast, we sprinkle the top with flake sea salt.

1 recipe Basic Pie Dough (page 213), rolled into 1 round

½ cup (4 oz/125 g) unsalted butter, melted and cooled

¾ cup (3½ oz/105 g) firmly packed light brown sugar

2 tablespoons cornstarch

Pinch of kosher salt

1 teaspoon pure vanilla extract

¾ cup (9 oz/280 g) honey

3 large eggs, lightly beaten

½ cup (125 ml) heavy cream

2 teaspoons fresh lemon juice

Flake sea salt, for sprinkling

SERVES 8-10

Make the pie dough. Fit the dough round into a 9-inch (23-cm) deep-dish pie dish. Trim the overhang to ½ inch (12 mm), fold the edge under itself, and decoratively flute or crimp. Freeze for 30 minutes.

Meanwhile, preheat the oven to 350°F (180°C).

Line the crust with aluminum foil and fill with pie weights. Bake until lightly browned and dry to the touch, about 20 minutes. Remove the foil and weights and set on a wire rack to cool completely. Keep the oven set.

In a large bowl, stir together the melted butter, brown sugar, cornstarch, salt, vanilla, honey, eggs, cream, and lemon juice. Pour the filling into the crust.

Bake until puffed and golden brown, 45–50 minutes, covering the edges with aluminum foil if they brown too quickly. Let cool completely on a wire rack before serving. Sprinkle with flake sea salt and serve.

TIP *Choose a honey that is flavorful but not overpowering, such as wildflower or clover.*

Peanut Butter Pie with Pretzel Crust

The beloved combination of peanut butter and chocolate is updated with a lightly salty pretzel crust. Be sure to use creamy peanut butter (or another favorite creamy nut butter) to retain the smooth texture of the pie.

1 recipe Pretzel Crust (page 215), baked and cooled

1½ cups (375 ml) heavy cream

½ lb (250 g) cream cheese, at room temperature

½ cup (2 oz/60 g) confectioners' sugar

¼ teaspoon kosher salt

1 teaspoon pure vanilla extract

1¼ cups (12½ oz/390 g) creamy peanut butter

1 recipe Whipped Cream (page 225)

Melted chocolate and chopped peanut butter cups, for garnish

SERVES 8-10

Make the pretzel crust.

In the bowl of a stand mixer fitted with the whisk attachment, beat the cream on medium speed until soft peaks form, 4–5 minutes. Transfer to a bowl.

In the same mixer bowl using the paddle attachment, beat the cream cheese on medium speed until smooth and pliable, about 3 minutes. Add the confectioners' sugar, salt, and vanilla and beat until well combined, 1–2 minutes. Add the peanut butter and beat until smooth, 1–2 minutes.

Using a rubber spatula, fold the reserved whipped cream into the peanut butter mixture until incorporated, 2–3 minutes; be careful not to overmix.

Pour the filling into the crust. Refrigerate for at least 2 hours or up to overnight before serving. Top with whipped cream and garnish with melted chocolate and chopped peanut butter cups.

TIP *Other types of nut butters, such as almond or cashew, would also be delicious.*

Pumpkin Chai Mini Pies

Pumpkin pie doesn't have to be only for the Thanksgiving table. Update this classic for your next autumn or winter dinner party by making sweet little individual pies with the warm, fragrant flavors of chai: cinnamon, ginger, cardamom, and cloves.

2 recipes Basic Pie Dough (page 213), rolled into 2 rounds

Nonstick cooking spray

1 can (15 oz/470 g) pumpkin purée

1 cup (7 oz/220 g) firmly packed light brown sugar

1 tablespoon cornstarch

¾ teaspoon cinnamon

¾ teaspoon ground ginger

½ teaspoon ground cardamom

½ teaspoon ground cloves

½ teaspoon kosher salt

3 large eggs, lightly beaten

1 cup (250 ml) heavy cream

1¼ teaspoons pure vanilla extract

1 recipe Whipped Cream (page 225), for serving

MAKES 24 MINI PIES

Make the pie dough. Lightly coat 24 standard muffin cups with nonstick cooking spray. Using a 4-inch (10-cm) round cutter, cut out 24 rounds and fit them into the prepared muffin cups, gathering the scraps of dough and rerolling as needed. Trim the edges, if necessary, leaving a ¼-inch (6-mm) overhang. Freeze for 30 minutes.

Meanwhile, preheat the oven to 350°F (180°C).

Bake the crusts until dry to the touch and lightly browned, about 20 minutes. Let cool completely on wire racks. Keep the oven set.

In a large bowl, whisk together the pumpkin purée and brown sugar. Add the cornstarch, cinnamon, ginger, cardamom, cloves, and salt and whisk until smooth. Add the eggs and whisk until combined. Add the cream and vanilla and whisk until smooth. Divide the filling among the crusts.

Bake until the filling is set, 30–35 minutes, covering the edges with aluminum foil if they brown too quickly. Let cool completely on wire racks before serving. Serve each mini pie with a dollop of whipped cream.

TIP *Replace the cardamom with ¼ teaspoon ground nutmeg for a more traditional pumpkin pie flavor profile.*

Plum Galette with Almond Filling

A galette, stemming from the Norman French word *gale*, which means "flat cake," refers to any free-form crusty cake. In this version, the single crust is folded partway over the filling. It's a wonderful after-dinner treat, especially when accompanied by a glass of port.

FOR THE CRUST

1½ cups (6½ oz/185 g) all-purpose flour, plus more for dusting

2 tablespoons granulated sugar

1 teaspoon kosher salt

¾ cup (6 oz/170 g) cold unsalted butter, cut into ¼-inch (6-mm) pieces

⅓ cup (80 ml) ice water

FOR THE ALMOND FILLING

½ cup (2½ oz/70 g) blanched almonds

⅓ cup (2½ oz/70 g) granulated sugar

4 tablespoons (2 oz/60 g) unsalted butter, cut into 4 pieces, at room temperature

1 large egg, at room temperature

1 tablespoon almond flour

1 teaspoon pure vanilla extract

½ teaspoon kosher salt

2 lb (1 kg) plums, pitted and cut into ¼-inch (6-mm) slices

⅓ cup (2½ oz/70 g) granulated sugar

2 tablespoons cornstarch

2 tablespoons fresh lemon juice

1 tablespoon heavy cream

2 tablespoons turbinado sugar

SERVES 10

Line a baking sheet with parchment paper.

To make the crust, in a large bowl, whisk the flour, granulated sugar, and salt. Add the butter and toss to coat with the flour mixture. Using your fingers, rub the butter pieces into the flour until no chunks of butter remain, only small, shaggy, flat pieces. Take care not to overmix; there should still be visible pieces of butter. Drizzle in the ice water and stir with a rubber spatula until the dough mostly comes together; it will be dry, shaggy, and loose.

Turn the dough out onto a lightly floured work surface and press together to form a mass, gathering up as many loose pieces as possible. Using a rolling pin, roll out and shape the dough into a round about ½ inch (12 mm) thick. Then fold the dough in half and reshape into a round about the same size. Repeat this process 3 more times, reshaping into a round each time and ending with a round about 6 inches (15 cm) in diameter and ½ inch (12 mm) thick.

Pick up the dough round and flour the surface well. Using a floured rolling pin, roll out the dough into a 14-inch (35-cm) round. Brush any excess flour off the dough. Place the rolling pin on one edge of the dough round and carefully roll up the dough. Transfer to the prepared baking sheet and unroll so the round is flat. It's okay if it hangs slightly over the edges of the baking sheet. Refrigerate the dough while you prepare the filling.

Preheat the oven to 375°F (190°C).

To make the almond filling, in a food processor, combine the almonds and granulated sugar and process until finely ground. Add the butter, egg, almond flour, vanilla, and salt and process until smooth. Spoon the filling over the dough, leaving a 2-inch (5-cm) border uncovered along the edge.

In a large bowl, toss together the plums, granulated sugar, cornstarch, and lemon juice. Arrange the plums on the filling, slightly overlapping them as needed; discard any juices in the bowl. Carefully fold the dough up and over the filling and plums, pleating the dough loosely and leaving the filling uncovered in the center. Brush the edges of the dough with the cream and sprinkle with the turbinado sugar.

Bake until the filling is puffed up slightly and set, the plums have released their juices, and the crust is golden brown, 45–50 minutes. Let cool on a wire rack for at least 15 minutes before serving.

Caramelized Leek & Green Onion Galette with Goat Cheese

This flaky crust is an excellent foundation for the savory onions and tangy goat cheese. Adding ice cold water is crucial—it slows down the yeast fermentation process and prevents bubbles from forming in the dough, which make it prone to tearing.

FOR THE CRUST

1½ cups (6½ oz/185 g) all-purpose flour, plus more for dusting

1 tablespoon sugar

2½ teaspoons kosher salt

¾ cup (6 oz/170 g) cold unsalted butter, cut into ¼-inch (6-mm) pieces

⅓ cup (80 ml) ice water

FOR THE CARAMELIZED LEEKS AND ONIONS

4 tablespoons (2 oz/60 g) unsalted butter

3 tablespoons extra-virgin olive oil

1 yellow onion, thinly sliced

3 leeks, white parts only, halved, rinsed, and thinly sliced

3 green onions, white and pale green parts only, thinly sliced

5 cloves garlic, thinly sliced

Kosher salt and freshly ground pepper

2 tablespoons Dijon mustard

1 large egg white beaten with 1 tablespoon water

Flaky sea salt

¼ lb (115 g) crumbled goat cheese, at room temperature

Balsamic vinegar, for drizzling

SERVES 10

To make the crust, in a large bowl, whisk the flour, sugar, and kosher salt. Add the butter and toss to coat with the flour mixture. Using your fingers, rub the butter pieces into the flour until no chunks of butter remain, only small, flat, shaggy pieces. Take care not to overmix; there should still be visible pieces of butter. Drizzle in the ice water and stir with a rubber spatula until the dough mostly comes together; it will be dry, shaggy, and loose.

Turn the dough out onto a lightly floured work surface and press together to form a mass, gathering up as many loose pieces as possible. Using a rolling pin, roll out and shape the dough into a round about ½ inch (12 mm) thick. Then fold the dough in half and reshape into a round about the same size. Repeat this process 3 more times, reshaping into a round each time and ending with a round about 6 inches (15 cm) in diameter and ½ inch (12 mm) thick.

Pick up the dough round and flour the surface well. Using a floured rolling pin, roll out the dough into a 14-inch (35-cm) round. Brush any excess flour off the dough. Place the rolling pin on one edge of the dough round and carefully roll up the dough. Transfer to the prepared baking sheet and unroll so the round is flat. It's okay if it hangs slightly over the edges of the baking sheet. Refrigerate the dough while you prepare the leek mixture.

Preheat the oven to 375°F (190°C).

To make the caramelized leeks and onions, in a large frying pan over medium heat, melt the butter with the oil. Add the yellow onion, leeks, green onions, and garlic and cook, stirring frequently, for 5 minutes, until softened. Reduce the heat to low and cook, stirring occasionally, until the mixture is cooked down and dark brown and caramelized, 25–30 minutes. Season to taste with kosher salt and pepper. Remove from the heat.

Brush the mustard over the dough, leaving a 2-inch (5-cm) border uncovered along the edge. Top with the leek mixture, spreading evenly. Carefully fold the dough up and over the filling, pleating the dough loosely and leaving the filling uncovered in the center. Brush the edges of the dough with the egg mixture and sprinkle with sea salt and pepper.

Bake until the crust is deep golden brown and the filling is caramelized, 40 minutes. Remove from the oven and dollop the cheese over the filling. Continue to bake until the cheese is softened and warm and the crust is golden brown, about 10 minutes longer. Drizzle with balsamic vinegar and serve warm or at room temperature. Let cool on a wire rack for at least 15 minutes before serving.

Vegetable Potpie
with Herbed Biscuits

This hearty potpie is chock full of seasonal autumn root vegetables, but feel free to trade in your own favorites depending upon what you have on hand. Sweet potatoes, winter squash, or even broccoli would all be great additions.

3 large carrots

2 Yukon gold potatoes

1 parsnip

1 celery root

1 fennel bulb, sliced

2 teaspoons olive oil

1 yellow onion, finely chopped

Kosher salt and freshly ground black pepper

1 cup (5 oz/155 g) thawed frozen peas

6 tablespoons (3 oz/90 g) unsalted butter

¼ cup (1½ oz/45 g) all-purpose flour

2 cups (500 ml) vegetable broth

1½ cups (6 oz/185 g) grated Gruyère cheese

¼ teaspoon each ground nutmeg and cayenne pepper

1 recipe Herbed Biscuit Dough (page 216)

Flake sea salt, for sprinkling

SERVES 6–8

Peel the carrots, potatoes, parsnip, and celery root and cut into ½-inch (12-mm) pieces and put into a large saucepan. Add the fennel and 1 inch (2.5 cm) of water. Cover and cook over medium heat until the vegetables are tender, 10–12 minutes. Drain well.

Meanwhile, in a sauté pan over medium heat, warm the oil. Add the onion and a pinch of kosher salt and stir occasionally until lightly caramelized, 6–8 minutes. Transfer to a large bowl. Add the cooked vegetables and toss with a generous pinch of kosher salt. Add the peas and toss to combine. Transfer to a large Dutch oven or a 9-by-13-inch (23-by-33-cm) baking dish.

Preheat the oven to 425°F (220°C).

In a saucepan over medium heat, melt 4 tablespoons (2 oz/60 g) of the butter, then add the flour all at once and cook, whisking constantly, until deep golden brown, about 3 minutes. Add ½ cup (125 ml) of the broth and stir until completely incorporated. Repeat with the remaining broth, ½ cup (125 ml) at a time, then stir occasionally until the sauce thickens, about 4 minutes. Stir in the cheese, nutmeg, and cayenne and season with kosher salt and black pepper. Pour the sauce over the vegetables and gently stir to coat.

Make the herbed dough. Bake until the biscuit top is golden brown and cooked through, 15–20 minutes. Melt the remaining 2 tablespoons butter. Brush the top with the butter and sprinkle with the flake sea salt. Serve warm.

TIP *Sautéed mushrooms add a wonderful earthy note to this hearty vegetarian dish, which can also be baked in individual cocottes or ramekins.*

Chicken Potpie with Mushrooms & Thyme

Feed a crowd with this delicious, hefty pie. We love the look and texture of filo dough (which can be found in the freezer section at supermarkets), but you can also use puff pastry or even pie dough for the top. Just bake it until bubbly and the crust is nicely browned.

4 ribs celery

1 lb (500 g) cremini mushrooms

½ lb (250 g) small potatoes

¾ cup (6 oz/185 g) plus 2 tablespoons unsalted butter

1 cup (5 oz/155 g) plus 2 tablespoons all-purpose flour

⅓ cup (80 ml) Madeira

2 tablespoons chicken demi-glace

7 cups (1.75 l) chicken broth

1 large yellow onion, diced

1 tablespoon chopped fresh thyme

2 teaspoons chopped fresh tarragon

1 bay leaf

8 cups cubed cooked chicken (about 3 lb/1.5 kg total)

1 bag (1 lb/500 g) thawed frozen pearl onions

Kosher salt and freshly ground pepper

1 recipe Filo Dough Top (page 216)

1 large egg beaten with 1 teaspoon water

Sea salt, for sprinkling

SERVES 8-10

Preheat the oven to 400°F (200°C).

Cut the celery into slices ⅛ inch (3 mm) thick. Brush clean and thinly slice the mushrooms. Cut the potatoes into ½-inch (12-mm) dice. In a large 5-qt (5-l) Dutch oven over medium heat, melt the butter. Add the flour and cook, stirring constantly, until the mixture smells fragrant and nutty, about 2 minutes. Whisk in the Madeira and demi-glace. Slowly add the broth, whisking until smooth, and bring to a boil. Add the yellow onion, celery, mushrooms, thyme, tarragon, and bay leaf and cook, stirring occasionally, until the vegetables are almost tender, about 10 minutes. Add the potatoes, chicken, and pearl onions and season with kosher salt and pepper. Cook until the potatoes are tender, about 10 minutes. Let cool for 10 minutes. Discard the bay leaf.

Make the filo dough top.

Carefully lift the stack of buttered filo and place it on top of the chicken mixture, folding the dough up as necessary along the edges of the pot. Brush the filo with the egg mixture and sprinkle with sea salt.

Bake until bubbly and the filo is crisp and browned all over, 15–20 minutes, covering the edges with aluminum foil if they brown too quickly. Let cool for about 10 minutes before serving.

TIP *For a delicious variation, replace the filo with an Herbed Biscuit Dough (see page 216).*

Bacon, Cheddar & Potato Hot Pockets

These savory hand pies are worlds apart from anything you could ever purchase in a store, and they are perfect for tucking into lunch boxes or taking on the road. Choose a good-quality thick-cut bacon for the best flavor.

1 recipe Cream Cheese Dough (page 216)

1 lb (500 g) Yukon gold potatoes, peeled and cut into ½-inch (12-mm) dice

Kosher salt and freshly ground pepper

½ cup (2½ oz/75 g) thawed frozen peas

6 oz (185 g) thick-cut bacon, cooked until crispy and roughly chopped

3 tablespoons unsalted butter

3 tablespoons all-purpose flour

1½ cups (375 ml) whole milk

1 cup (4 oz/125 g) grated Cheddar cheese, plus more for sprinkling

1 teaspoon Dijon mustard

1 large egg beaten with 1 teaspoon water

MAKES 6 HOT POCKETS

Make the cream cheese dough. Preheat the oven to 400°F (200°C). Line a baking sheet with parchment paper.

On a floured work surface, roll out the dough into a 15-by-16-inch (38-by-40-cm) rectangle about ¼ inch (6 mm) thick. Cut into 12 rectangles, each 4 by 5 inches (10 by 13 cm). Place the rectangles on the prepared baking sheet and refrigerate until ready to use.

Put the potatoes in a saucepan with 1 inch (2.5 cm) of water, cover, and cook over medium heat until the potatoes are tender, about 10 minutes. Drain well, transfer to a large bowl, and toss with 1 teaspoon salt, the peas, and bacon.

In a saucepan over medium heat, melt the butter, then add the flour all at once and cook, whisking constantly, until deep golden brown, about 3 minutes. Add ½ cup (125 ml) of the milk and stir until completely incorporated. Repeat with the remaining milk, ½ cup (125 ml) at a time, then stir occasionally until the sauce thickens, about 2 minutes. Stir in the cheese and mustard and season with salt and pepper. Pour the sauce over the potato filling and gently stir to coat. Let cool to lukewarm.

On the baking sheet, space 6 of the dough rectangles at least 1 inch (2.5 cm) apart. Brush them with some of the egg mixture, then place about ⅓ cup (1¾ oz/55 g) of the filling in the center of each. Top each with a remaining dough rectangle. Press the top and bottom rectangle edges together, then crimp with a fork. Brush the tops with the egg mixture and cut small steam vents in each.

Bake until the crusts are golden brown, 18–20 minutes, and during the last 5 minutes of baking, sprinkle cheese over the tops of the pockets, and serve warm.

TIP *If you have dough scraps, gather them up and reroll to make more hot pockets.*

Shepherd's Pie

Here, a hearty filling of ground beef, carrots, peas, and herbs is topped with creamy mounds of buttery mashed potatoes. Drag the tines of a fork across the mash to give it texture, then dot a few small pieces of butter over the top to help it brown up nicely.

2 lb (1 kg) russet potatoes

2 tablespoons olive oil

2 lb (1 kg) ground beef

Kosher salt and freshly ground pepper

1 yellow onion

3 large carrots, peeled and cut into ½-inch (12-mm) pieces

3 ribs celery, cut into ½-inch (12-mm) pieces

2 cloves garlic, minced

⅔ cup (160 ml) white wine

1½ cups (375 ml) chicken or beef broth

2 teaspoons tomato paste

1½ teaspoons Worcestershire sauce

1 teaspoon Dijon mustard

1 tablespoon finely chopped fresh rosemary or thyme

1 cup (5 oz/155 g) frozen peas

4 tablespoons (2 oz/60 g) unsalted butter

1¼ cups (310 ml) half-and-half

½ teaspoon ground nutmeg

½ cup (2 oz/60 g) grated Parmesan cheese

SERVES 6–8

Peel and quarter the potatoes. In a saucepan over high heat, bring the potatoes to a boil in salted water. Reduce the heat and simmer until the potatoes are tender, 20–25 minutes. Drain and keep warm.

Meanwhile, in a large sauté pan over medium-high heat, warm 1 tablespoon of the oil. Add the beef and season with salt and pepper. Stir occasionally until browned, 7–10 minutes. Transfer to a bowl and discard excess fat from the pan.

Meanwhile, finely chop the onion. In the same pan over medium-low heat, warm the remaining 1 tablespoon oil. Add the onion and a pinch of salt and stir occasionally until caramelized, about 10 minutes. Add the carrots, celery, and garlic and stir occasionally until the carrots are just tender, about 5 minutes. Raise the heat to medium-high, add the wine, and simmer until reduced by half, about 5 minutes. Stir in the broth, tomato paste, Worcestershire sauce, mustard, and ½ tablespoon of the rosemary. Stir occasionally until slightly thickened, 6–8 minutes. Add the peas during the last minute of cooking. Return the beef to the pan. Season with salt and pepper. Remove the pan from the heat and cover to keep warm.

Place a rack in the upper third of the oven and preheat to 375°F (190°C). Transfer the potatoes to a large bowl and mash with a potato masher. Add the butter and half-and-half and stir until the mixture is well blended. Stir in the nutmeg and season with salt and pepper.

Spread the filling evenly in a 9-by-13-inch (23-by-33-cm) or 5-qt (5-l) capacity baking dish. Spread the mashed potatoes evenly on top. Sprinkle with the cheese and the remaining ½ tablespoon rosemary. Bake until the potatoes are lightly browned, 15–20 minutes. Let cool for 5 minutes, then serve warm.

TIP *This dish is naturally gluten-free, but for a thicker sauce, stir ⅓ cup (2 oz/60 g) flour into the filling when you add the beef back in.*

Quiche with Leeks, Goat Cheese & Fresh Herbs

We love the versatility of quiche, and this is one of our favorite versions. Filled with buttery leeks, plenty of herbs, and tangy goat cheese, it makes a terrific brunch dish or a light lunch when served with a green salad.

1 recipe Cream Cheese Dough (page 216)

1 tablespoon unsalted butter

1 tablespoon olive oil

3 leeks, white and pale green parts, rinsed and thinly sliced

Kosher salt and freshly ground pepper

4 large eggs

1½ cups (375 ml) whole milk

¼ teaspoon ground nutmeg

1 tablespoon chopped fresh dill

1 tablespoon chopped fresh flat-leaf parsley

½ bunch green onions, white and pale green parts thinly sliced

6 oz (185 g) goat cheese, crumbled

SERVES 8

Make the cream cheese dough. On a well-floured work surface, roll out the dough into a 12-inch (30-cm) round and fit into a 9-inch (23-cm) pie dish. Trim the overhang to ½ inch (12 mm), fold the edge under itself, and decoratively flute or crimp. Pierce the bottom of the crust with a fork and freeze for 30 minutes.

Meanwhile, preheat the oven to 400°F (200°C).

Bake the crust until the edges are lightly browned, about 15 minutes. Let cool briefly on a wire rack. Reduce the oven temperature to 375°F (190°C).

In a sauté pan over medium heat, melt the butter with the oil. Add the leeks and ½ teaspoon salt and stir occasionally until the leeks are tender and translucent, about 10 minutes. Let cool slightly.

In a large bowl, whisk the eggs until blended. Whisk in the milk, ½ teaspoon salt, ¼ teaspoon pepper, the nutmeg, dill, parsley, and green onions. Stir in the leeks and half of the cheese. Sprinkle the remaining cheese over the crust, then pour in the egg mixture.

Bake until the crust is golden brown and the filling is set and slightly puffed, 30–35 minutes, covering the edges with aluminum foil if they brown too quickly. Let cool briefly on a wire rack, then cut the quiche into wedges and serve warm.

TIP *Customize this quiche as you wish—swap in your favorite cheese or vegetables, add ham or cooked bacon, or try other herbs and spices.*

Tamale Mini Pies

These spicy little pies, filled with chile-spiked chorizo, beef, tomatoes, black beans, and corn, make a great weeknight meal. Prep the filling up to 2 days ahead, then stir up the corn bread topping at the last minute before baking.

3 tablespoons olive oil

¼ lb (125 g) fresh Mexican chorizo

½ lb (250 g) ground beef

½ yellow onion, diced

1 jalapeño chile, seeded and diced

2 cloves garlic, minced

1 teaspoon ground cumin

1 teaspoon dried oregano

1 teaspoon chili powder

Pinch of red pepper flakes

Kosher salt and freshly ground black pepper

1 can (14 oz/440 g) diced tomatoes with juices

1 cup (250 ml) chicken or beef broth

2 tablespoons tomato paste

1 can (15 oz/470 g) black beans

1½ cups (9 oz/280 g) fresh or thawed frozen corn kernels

1 recipe Corn Bread Topping (page 215)

SERVES 6-8

Preheat the oven to 350°F (180°C).

In a large sauté pan over medium heat, warm 2 tablespoons of the oil. Add the chorizo and ground beef and stir occasionally until browned and cooked through, 6–8 minutes. Transfer to a bowl. Discard any excess fat from the pan.

In the same pan over medium-high heat, warm the remaining 1 tablespoon oil. Add the onion and jalapeño and cook, stirring occasionally, until soft and translucent, 2–3 minutes. Add the garlic and stir for 30 seconds. Add the cumin, oregano, chili powder, red pepper flakes, and a large pinch each of salt and black pepper. Add the tomatoes and their juices, broth, tomato paste, black beans, corn, and the browned meats. Stir well to combine and season with salt and pepper. Divide among 6–8 eight-ounce cocottes or ramekins. Place on a baking sheet.

Make the corn bread topping. Spoon the topping on top of the filled cocottes.

Bake until the corn bread topping is cooked through and golden brown, about 30 minutes. Serve right away.

TIP *If you don't have cocottes, transfer the mixture to a 9-inch (23-cm) square baking dish and bake as directed.*

BREADS

Popovers

An American classic, popovers are so named because they "pop" over the pan during baking, thanks to the eggs in the batter. Resist the urge to take a peek while the popovers are baking; opening the oven door prematurely will cause them to deflate.

1½ cups (350 ml) whole milk

3 tablespoons unsalted butter

3 large eggs, at room temperature

1 cup (4 oz/115 g) all-purpose flour

3 tablespoons sugar

1 teaspoon kosher salt

Nonstick cooking spray

Salted butter, for serving

Jam, for serving

MAKES 6 POPOVERS

Place a rack in the lower third of the oven. Set a 6-cup popover pan on a baking sheet and place in the oven. Preheat the oven to 450°F (230°C).

In a small saucepan over medium-high heat, combine the milk and unsalted butter. Bring to a simmer, whisking occasionally until the milk is hot and the butter melts, about 5 minutes. Remove from the heat and let cool slightly.

In a large bowl, whisk the eggs until smooth and light in color. While whisking constantly, very slowly pour in half of the warm milk mixture, taking care not to curdle the eggs. Then slowly add the remaining milk and whisk until combined. Sift the flour, sugar, and salt over the egg mixture and whisk until only a few small lumps remain, taking care not to overmix. Transfer the batter to a large liquid measuring cup or other container with a spout.

Carefully remove the baking sheet and popover pan from the oven. Generously coat the popover wells with nonstick cooking spray. Divide the batter among the wells, filling each about three-fourths full.

Bake for 20 minutes, then reduce the oven temperature to 350°F (180°C). Continue to bake until the popovers are puffed over the pan and are deep brown and dry to the touch, about 25 minutes longer.

Let the popovers cool for 3 minutes, then serve warm with salted butter and jam.

Sour Cream Coffee Cake

The streusel topping lends a crumbly, slightly crunchy texture to this light cake. Coffee is its tried-and-true partner, but a piping hot cup of Earl Grey or English breakfast tea is delightful as well.

FOR THE CAKE

Nonstick cooking spray

3 cups (12 oz/340 g) all-purpose flour

1½ teaspoons kosher salt

1 teaspoon baking powder

1 teaspoon baking soda

1 cup (8 oz/225 g) unsalted butter, at room temperature

1⅓ cups (9½ oz/270 g) granulated sugar

2 large eggs, at room temperature

1 tablespoon vanilla bean paste

1¼ cups (10 oz/285 g) sour cream

FOR THE STREUSEL

2 cups (9 oz/250 g) all-purpose flour

1 cup (4 oz/115 g) chopped toasted pecans (optional)

1 cup (7½ oz/210 g) firmly packed light brown sugar

1 cup (8 oz/225 g) unsalted butter, melted and cooled

1 tablespoon plus 1 teaspoon ground cinnamon

1⅛ teaspoons kosher salt

Makes one 9-by-13-inch (23-by-33-cm) cake;
SERVES 8

To make the cake, preheat the oven to 350°F (180°C). Lightly coat a 9-by-13-inch (23-by-33-cm) baking dish with nonstick cooking spray.

In a bowl, whisk together the flour, salt, baking powder, and baking soda. Set aside.

In the bowl of a stand mixer fitted with the paddle attachment, beat the butter on medium-high speed until smooth, about 2 minutes. Add the granulated sugar and beat until very light and fluffy, about 3 minutes. (Don't skimp out on the time here.)

Reduce the speed to low, add the eggs one at a time, and vanilla, and beat until just combined, about 1 minute. Raise the speed to high and beat until very smooth and silky, about 1 minute. Stop the mixer and scrape down the sides of the bowl. Add the flour mixture in 3 additions, alternating with the sour cream and beginning and ending with the flour, and beat on medium speed until smooth, about 3 minutes. Raise the speed to medium-high and beat for 30 seconds. Transfer the batter to the prepared dish and spread evenly.

To make the streusel, in a bowl, stir together the flour, pecans (if using), brown sugar, melted butter, cinnamon, and salt until a wet, crumbly mixture forms. Using your hands, break up the streusel and sprinkle it over the batter, gently pressing it down onto the surface.

Bake until a toothpick inserted into the center of the cake comes out clean and the streusel is deep golden brown, 47–50 minutes. Allow to cool for 10 minutes, then cut and serve warm.

Cinnamon Rolls with Cream Cheese Frosting

These pastries are tailor-made for a lazy Sunday brunch: you can prepare the dough a day ahead and let it rise overnight in the refrigerator. Then let the rolls warm up and allow them to rise further, until doubled in size from their original shape, before baking.

FOR THE DOUGH

¾ cup (180 ml) warm whole milk (110°F/43°C)

1 package (2¼ teaspoons) active dry yeast

¼ cup (1¾ oz/50 g) plus 1 tablespoon granulated sugar

1 large egg plus 1 large egg yolk, at room temperature

4 tablespoons (2 oz/60 g) unsalted butter, melted and cooled

3 cups (12 oz/340 g) plus 1 tablespoon bread flour, plus more for dusting

¾ teaspoon kosher salt

Canola oil, for greasing

FOR THE FILLING

¾ cup (5½ oz/155 g) firmly packed dark brown sugar

2 tablespoons ground cinnamon

¼ teaspoon kosher salt

6 tablespoons (3 oz/90 g) unsalted butter, cut into pieces, at room temperature

2 teaspoons vanilla bean paste

MAKES 11 ROLLS

To make the dough, in the bowl of a stand mixer, whisk together the warm milk, yeast, and the 1 tablespoon granulated sugar. Let stand until foamy, about 10 minutes. Add the ¼ cup (1¾ oz/50 g) granulated sugar, egg, egg yolk, and melted butter. Fit the mixer with the paddle attachment and beat on low speed until just combined, about 2 minutes. Add the flour and salt and beat until a wet dough forms, about 10 seconds. Switch to the dough hook and knead on medium speed until the dough is smooth and elastic and only slightly sticky, about 10 minutes.

Turn the dough out onto a work surface and knead once or twice. Shape the dough into a ball and place in a well-oiled large bowl, turning to coat the dough with the oil. Cover the bowl with plastic wrap and a kitchen towel and let the dough rise in a warm spot until doubled in size, 1–1½ hours.

Meanwhile, make the filling: In the clean bowl of the stand mixer fitted with the clean paddle attachment, beat together the brown sugar, cinnamon, salt, butter, and vanilla on medium speed until a smooth paste forms, about 1 minute. Transfer to a bowl and set aside.

Butter a 12-inch (30-cm) ovenproof frying pan. Turn the dough out onto a well-floured work surface. Sprinkle lightly with flour and roll out into a rectangle 14 by 11 inches (35 by 28 cm), with a short side toward you.

Dollop the filling over the dough. Using an offset spatula, spread evenly, leaving a ¼-inch (6-mm) border on the short side farthest from you. Starting from the side closest to you, roll the dough tightly into a log, brushing off the excess flour as you go. Pinch the seams to seal. Reshape as needed so the log is 11 inches (28 cm) long. Using a serrated knife, cut the log crosswise into 11 slices, each 1 inch (2.5 cm) wide.

Continued on page 177

Continued from page 174

FOR THE CREAM CHEESE FROSTING

¼ cup (2 oz/60 g) cream cheese, at room temperature

4 tablespoons (2 oz/60 g) unsalted butter, at room temperature

¾ cup (3 oz/90 g) confectioners' sugar

1 teaspoon vanilla bean paste

⅛ teaspoon kosher salt

Place the rolls in the prepared frying pan. Cover the pan with plastic wrap and a kitchen towel, and let the rolls rise in warm spot until doubled in size, about 1 hour.

Preheat the oven to 350°F (180°C).

Remove the towel and plastic wrap from the pan. Bake until the rolls are golden brown, 20–23 minutes. You want them to be slightly underbaked.

While the rolls are baking, make the cream cheese frosting: In the clean bowl of the stand mixer fitted with the clean paddle attachment, beat together the cream cheese and butter on medium speed until smooth, about 1 minute. Add the confectioners' sugar, vanilla, and salt and beat on low speed until combined, about 2 minutes. Raise the speed to medium-high and beat until light and fluffy, about 1 minute.

Transfer the pan to a wire rack and let cool for 10 minutes, then spread the rolls with the cream cheese frosting. Serve warm or at room temperature.

Chocolate Chip Banana Bread

If you'd like, sprinkle chopped walnuts over the top of the loaf before baking to give this bread a satisfying crunch. For a double-chocolate banana loaf, swap in ¼ cup (¾ oz/20 g) unsweetened cocoa powder for ¼ cup (1 oz/30 g) of the all-purpose flour.

½ cup (4 oz/115 g) unsalted butter, at room temperature, plus more for greasing

1¾ cups (7½ oz/210 g) all-purpose flour, plus more for dusting

1 teaspoon baking soda

½ teaspoon baking powder

¼ teaspoon kosher salt

1 cup (7 oz/200 g) sugar

2 large eggs, at room temperature

1 teaspoon pure vanilla extract

3 very ripe bananas, mashed (12 oz/340 g)

½ cup (3 oz/90 g) semisweet chocolate chips, plus more for sprinkling

Makes one 9-by-5-inch (23-by-13-cm) loaf or three 3½-by-6-inch (9-by-15-cm) loaves;

SERVES 6-8

Preheat the oven to 350°F (180°C). Butter and lightly flour a 9-by-5-inch (23-by-13-cm) loaf pan or three 3½-by-6-inch (9-by-15-cm) loaf pans.

In a bowl, sift together the flour, baking soda, baking powder, and salt. Set aside.

In the bowl of a stand mixer fitted with the paddle attachment, beat together the butter and sugar on medium speed until light and fluffy, about 3 minutes. Add the eggs one at a time, beating until incorporated after each addition, then add the vanilla and beat until smooth, about 1 minute. Reduce the speed to low, add the bananas, and beat until combined, about 30 seconds. Stop the mixer and scrape down the sides of the bowl. Add the flour mixture and beat on low speed just until the flour disappears, about 1 minute. Remove the bowl from the mixer. Using a rubber spatula, gently fold in the chocolate chips until evenly distributed. Pour the batter into the prepared pan(s) and spread evenly. Sprinkle with chocolate chips.

Bake until the bread is golden brown and a toothpick inserted into the center comes out clean, about 55 minutes for the large loaf and about 35 minutes for the small loaves.

Transfer the pan(s) to a wire rack and let cool for 15 minutes, then turn the bread out onto the rack and let cool completely. Cut into slices and serve.

Classic Scones

For flaky scones, the trick lies in the butter, which must be cold while handling. The layers that create the flakiness develop in the oven once the cold butter melts. These pair beautifully with your favorite jam, curds, or clotted cream.

2 large eggs

½ cup (120 ml) cold buttermilk

3 cups (12 oz/340 g) all-purpose flour, plus more for dusting

⅓ cup (2½ oz/70 g) plus 2 tablespoons sugar, plus more for sprinkling

1½ teaspoons baking powder

¼ teaspoon fine sea salt

1 cup (8 oz/225 g) cold unsalted butter, cut into ½-inch (12-mm) pieces

1 tablespoon heavy cream

MAKES 8 SCONES

In a large bowl, lightly whisk the eggs until blended, then whisk in the buttermilk. Set aside.

In a food processor, combine the flour, sugar, baking powder, and salt and pulse until blended. Add the butter and pulse until moist, pea-size crumbs form. Take care not to overprocess as you don't want to combine the flour and butter too much.

Add the flour mixture to the egg mixture. Using your hands or a rubber spatula, quickly combine just until the dough comes together and looks shaggy.

Turn the dough out onto a lightly floured work surface and shape into a ball. If the dough is too crumbly to shape and cut, then knead a few times before shaping into a ball. Gently press down with the palm of your hand to flatten, then shape the dough into an 8-inch (20-cm) round. Using a bench scraper or a knife, cut the dough into 4 equal wedges and wrap separately in plastic wrap. Refrigerate for at least 15 minutes or up to overnight.

Preheat the oven to 400°F (200°C). Line a baking sheet with parchment paper.

Remove the plastic wrap from the dough. Using a bench scraper or a knife, cut each piece in half to form a total of 8 wedges, working quickly to ensure the butter stays cold. Transfer to the prepared baking sheet, spacing the scones evenly apart. Brush the tops of the scones with the cream and sprinkle generously with sugar.

Bake until the scones are lightly golden and a toothpick inserted into the center comes out clean, about 20 minutes.

Transfer the scones to a wire rack and let cool for at least 5 minutes before serving.

Herb & Parmesan Scones

Scones are best served fresh. If you want to prepare the dough ahead of time, you can store the precut pieces in the refrigerator up to overnight. Alternatively, cut the dough into 8 pieces, place them into an airtight container separated by parchment paper, and freeze for up to 1 month.

2 large eggs

2 cups (8 oz/225 g) grated Parmesan cheese, plus more for sprinkling

1 cup (8 oz/225 g) crème fraîche

3½ cups (14 oz/400 g) all-purpose flour, plus more for dusting

1½ teaspoons baking powder

1 teaspoon fine sea salt

¼ teaspoon freshly ground pepper, plus more for garnish

1 small pinch of ground nutmeg

1 cup (2 oz/60 g) chopped mixed fresh herbs, such as dill, rosemary, and thyme

1 cup (8 oz/225 g) cold unsalted butter, cut into ½-inch (12-mm) pieces

1 tablespoon heavy cream

MAKES 8 SCONES

In a large bowl, lightly whisk the eggs until blended, then whisk in the cheese and crème fraîche. Set aside.

In a food processer, combine the flour, baking powder, salt, pepper, nutmeg, and herbs and pulse until blended. Add the butter and pulse until moist, pea-size crumbs form. Take care not to overprocess as you don't want to combine the flour and butter too much.

Add the flour mixture to the egg mixture. Using your hands or a rubber spatula, quickly combine just until the dough comes together and looks shaggy.

Turn the dough out onto a lightly floured work surface, and quickly shape into a ball. If the dough is too crumbly to shape and cut, then knead a few times before shaping into a ball. Gently press down with the palm of your hand to flatten, then shape the dough into an 8-inch (20-cm) round. Using a bench scraper or a knife, cut the dough into 4 equal wedges and wrap separately in plastic wrap. Freeze for 30 minutes.

Preheat the oven to 400°F (200°C). Line a baking sheet with parchment paper.

Remove the plastic wrap from the dough. Using a bench scraper or a knife, and working quickly to ensure the butter stays cold, cut each piece in half to form a total of 8 wedges. Transfer to the prepared baking sheet, spacing the scones evenly apart. Brush the tops of the scones with the cream and sprinkle with cheese and pepper.

Bake until the scones are golden and a toothpick inserted into the center comes out clean, 20–25 minutes.

Transfer the scones to a wire rack and let cool for at least 5 minutes before serving.

TIP *Crème fraîche and prosciutto make excellent accompaniments to these savory pastries.*

Lemon–Poppy Seed Scones

A slathering of clotted cream and a side of berries make this the ideal weekend-morning treat. The scones can be cut and frozen for up to 1 month; if baking frozen dough, be sure to give the scones a few more minutes in the oven.

2 large eggs

½ cup (120 ml) cold buttermilk

½ cup (120 ml) plus 3 tablespoons fresh lemon juice

4¼ cups (17 oz/480 g) all-purpose flour, plus more for dusting

¾ cup (5 oz/140 g) granulated sugar

1½ teaspoons baking powder

½ teaspoon fine sea salt

3 tablespoons grated lemon zest, plus more for garnish

2 tablespoons poppy seeds

1 cup (8 oz/225 g) cold unsalted butter, cut into ½-inch (12-mm) pieces

1 tablespoon heavy cream

2 cups (8 oz/225 g) confectioners' sugar

MAKES 8 SCONES

In a large bowl, lightly whisk the eggs until blended, then whisk in the buttermilk and ¼ cup (60 ml) plus 3 tablespoons of the lemon juice. Set aside.

In a food processor, combine the flour, sugar, baking powder, salt, lemon zest, and poppy seeds and pulse until blended. Add the butter and pulse until moist, pea-size crumbs form, 8–10 pulses. Take care not to overprocess as you don't want to combine the flour and butter too much.

Add the flour mixture to the egg mixture. Using your hands or a rubber spatula, quickly combine just until the dough comes together and looks shaggy.

Turn the dough out onto a lightly floured work surface. Shape into a ball, working quickly to ensure the butter stays cold. If the dough is too crumbly to shape and cut, then knead a few times before shaping into a ball. Gently press down with the palm of your hand to flatten, then shape the dough into an 8-inch (20-cm) round. Using a bench scraper or a knife, cut the dough into 4 equal wedges and wrap separately in plastic wrap. Freeze for at least 30 minutes or refrigerate until butter has firmed.

Preheat the oven to 400°F (200°C). Line a baking sheet with parchment paper.

Remove the plastic wrap from the dough. Using a bench scraper or a knife, and working quickly to ensure the butter stays cold, cut each piece in half to form a total of 8 wedges. Transfer to the prepared baking sheet, spacing the scones evenly apart. Brush the tops of the scones with the cream.

Bake until the scones are golden and a toothpick inserted into the center comes out clean, 20–25 minutes.

Transfer the scones to a wire rack and let cool for 5 minutes.

Meanwhile, in a bowl, whisk together the confectioners' sugar and the remaining ¼ cup (60 ml) lemon juice. Drizzle the glaze over the warm scones and garnish with lemon zest. Let cool for 10 minutes longer before serving.

Cinnamon Monkey Bread

This classic pull-apart bread makes for a great shareable treat. If you don't have a Bundt pan, use an angel food cake pan or a tube pan—the central tube helps the bread to bake evenly.

FOR THE DOUGH

¾ cup (180 ml) warm whole milk (110°F/43°C)

1 package (2¼ teaspoons) active dry yeast

¼ cup (1¾ oz/50 g) plus 1 tablespoon granulated sugar

1 large egg plus 1 large egg yolk, at room temperature

4 tablespoons (2 oz/60 g) unsalted butter, melted and cooled, plus butter for greasing

3 cups (12 oz/340 g) plus 1 tablespoon bread flour, plus more for dusting

¾ teaspoon kosher salt

Nonstick cooking spray

FOR THE BROWN SUGAR COATING

1½ cups (11 oz/310 g) firmly packed light brown sugar

2½ tablespoons ground cinnamon

¾ cup (6 oz/170 g) unsalted butter, melted and cooled

FOR THE GLAZE

½ cup (2 oz/60 g) confectioners' sugar

1 tablespoon whole milk

1 teaspoon pure vanilla extract or vanilla bean paste

Pinch of kosher salt

SERVES 10-12

To make the dough, in the bowl of a stand mixer, whisk together the warm milk, yeast, and the 1 tablespoon granulated sugar. Let stand until foamy, about 10 minutes. Add the ¼ cup (1¾ oz/50 g) granulated sugar, egg, egg yolk, and melted butter. Fit the mixer with the paddle attachment and beat on low speed until just combined, about 2 minutes. Add the flour and salt and beat until a wet dough forms, about 10 seconds. Switch to the dough hook and knead on medium speed until the dough is smooth and elastic and only slightly sticky, about 10 minutes.

Coat a large bowl with nonstick cooking spray. Turn the dough out onto a work surface and knead once or twice. Shape the dough into a ball and place in the prepared bowl, turning to coat the dough with the oil. Cover the bowl with plastic wrap and a kitchen towel and let the dough rise in a warm spot until doubled in size, 1–1½ hours.

Meanwhile, make the brown sugar coating: In a bowl, stir together the brown sugar and cinnamon. Pour the melted butter into another bowl.

Generously butter a large Bundt pan. Turn the dough out onto a lightly floured work surface and gently pat into an 8-inch (20-cm) square. Using a lightly floured pastry cutter or knife, cut the dough into sixty-four 1-inch (2.5-cm) squares. Roll each into a ball, then dip in the melted butter and roll in the brown sugar mixture. Layer the balls in the prepared Bundt pan, staggering them so they aren't stacked directly on top of each other. This helps the bread to bake together in a puzzle structure.

Cover the pan with plastic wrap and let the dough rise in a warm spot until the balls are puffy and have risen at least 1 inch (2.5 cm) above the top of the pan, about 1 hour.

Preheat the oven to 350°F (180°C).

Remove the plastic wrap from the pan. Bake until the sugar on top caramelizes and the dough balls are firm to the touch, about 30 minutes. Transfer the pan to a wire rack and let cool for 5 minutes, then invert the bread onto a serving plate and let cool for 8–10 minutes longer.

Meanwhile, make the glaze: In a bowl, whisk together the confectioners' sugar, milk, vanilla, and salt until a smooth glaze forms. Pour over the warm bread and serve right away.

TIP *Don't let the bread cool in the pan for more than 5 minutes or it will stick to the pan and come out in pieces.*

Blueberry Muffins

To achieve a light and fluffy texture, don't skimp on the 2-minute creaming time—the beaters whip air into the butter, which causes the muffins to rise.

1½ cups (6½ oz/185 g) plus
1 teaspoon all-purpose flour

¾ teaspoon kosher salt

¾ teaspoon baking powder

½ teaspoon baking soda

1½ teaspoons ground cinnamon

½ cup (4 oz/115 g) unsalted
butter, at room temperature

¾ cup (5 oz/140 g)
granulated sugar

1 large egg, at room temperature

2 teaspoons pure vanilla extract

½ cup (4 oz/115 g) plus
2 tablespoons sour cream

1 pint (10 oz/285 g) fresh or
thawed frozen blueberries

¼ cup turbinado sugar

MAKES 12 MUFFINS

Preheat the oven to 375°F (190°C). Line 12 standard muffin cups with paper liners.

In a bowl, whisk together 1½ cups (6½ oz/185 g) flour, the salt, baking powder, baking soda, and cinnamon. Set aside.

In the bowl of a stand mixer fitted with the paddle attachment, beat the butter on medium speed until smooth, about 2 minutes. Add the granulated sugar and beat until very light and fluffy, about 3 minutes. Reduce the speed to low, add the egg and vanilla, and beat until just combined, about 1 minute. Raise the speed to high and beat until very smooth and silky, about 1 minute. Stop the mixer and scrape down the sides of the bowl. Add the flour mixture in 3 additions, alternating with the sour cream and beginning and ending with the flour, and beat on medium speed until smooth, about 3 minutes. Raise the speed to medium-high and beat for 30 seconds.

In a bowl, toss together the blueberries and the 1 teaspoon flour until coated. Remove the bowl from the mixer. Using a rubber spatula, gently fold the blueberries into the batter until evenly distributed. Divide the batter among the prepared muffin cups. Sprinkle each muffin with 1 teaspoon turbinado sugar.

Bake until a toothpick inserted into the center of a muffin comes out clean and the blueberries on the surface have just burst, 27–30 minutes. Let cool in muffin tin for 5 minutes, then turn out onto a wire rack to cool for 10 minutes longer, or until completely cooled.

Soft Pretzels with Sea Salt

Perfect for game day or movie night, these pretzels have endless potential for sweet and savory pairings, from icing to nacho cheese. Boiling them in baking-soda water before baking gives them their golden brown, crackled crust; although you can skip this step, you'll miss out on the pretzels' signature texture and appearance.

1 cup (240 ml) warm water (110°F/43°C)

1 package (2¼ teaspoons) active dry yeast

1 tablespoon sugar

6 tablespoons (3 oz/90 g) unsalted butter, melted and cooled

3¼ cups (13¾ oz/390 g) all-purpose flour, plus more for dusting

1½ teaspoons kosher salt

Canola oil, for brushing

7 cups (1.7 l) water

⅓ cup (2½ oz /75 g) baking soda

Flaky sea salt, for sprinkling

Dijon mustard, for serving

MAKES 6 LARGE PRETZELS

In the bowl of a stand mixer, whisk together the warm water, yeast, and sugar. Let stand until foamy, about 10 minutes. Add 3 tablespoons of the melted butter, the flour, and kosher salt. Fit the mixer with the dough hook and knead on medium-low speed until the dough is smooth and elastic, about 10 minutes.

Turn the dough out onto a work surface. Shape the dough into a ball and place in a lightly oiled large bowl, turning to coat the dough with the oil. Cover the bowl with plastic wrap and let the dough rise in a warm spot until doubled in size, about 1 hour.

Preheat the oven to 450°F (230°C).

Line 2 baking sheets with parchment paper and lightly brush the parchment with oil.

Turn the dough out onto a lightly floured work surface and cut into 6 equal pieces, each about 4 oz/120 g. Gently roll and stretch each piece into a rope about 24 inches (61 cm) long. Working with 1 rope at a time, position it horizontally, then bring the 2 ends up and toward the center as if forming an oval; cross one end over the other, twist the ends around each other, and then press the ends into the bottom of the oval to create a pretzel shape. Place the pretzels on the prepared baking sheets.

Pour the water into a large saucepan, whisk in the baking soda, and bring to a boil over high heat. Gently drop 2 pretzels at a time into the boiling water, taking care not to misshape them. Boil for 30 seconds, then use a large spider or large wooden spoon to flip the pretzels and boil for 20 seconds longer. Return the boiled pretzels, top side up, to the baking sheets, spacing them evenly apart. Sprinkle generously with sea salt.

Bake until the pretzels are golden brown, about 12 minutes, rotating the baking sheets between racks halfway through baking. Remove from the oven, brush the pretzels with the remaining 3 tablespoons melted butter, and continue to bake until the pretzels are deep golden brown and have a sheen, 2 minutes longer. Serve warm with Dijon mustard.

TIP *if you don't have a spider to turn the pretzels, you can use a large wooden spoon or tongs very gently so as not to morph the dough.*

Everything Bagels

Bagels are an excellent backdrop for other flavors. Although there's nothing quite like a bagel schmeared with cream cheese, you can elevate this classic combo by mincing any fresh herbs you have on hand and stirring them into the cheese.

1½ cups (350 ml) warm water (110°F/43°C)

2¾ teaspoons active dry yeast

4 cups (508 g) bread flour, plus more for dusting

1 tablespoon barley malt syrup

3 teaspoons kosher salt

Canola oil, for greasing

8 cups (1.9 l) water

¼ cup (3 oz/90 g) honey

1 cup (5 oz/145 g) everything bagel seasoning

1 large egg white beaten with 1 tablespoon water

Salted butter or cream cheese, for serving

MAKES 8 BAGELS

In the bowl of a stand mixer, whisk together the warm water and yeast. Let stand until foamy, about 10 minutes. Add the flour, barley malt syrup, and salt. Fit the mixer with the dough hook and beat on low speed until just combined, about 2 minutes. Raise the speed to medium and knead until the dough is sticky and elastic, about 3 minutes.

Scrape the dough out onto a well-floured work surface. Using well-floured hands, knead the dough until smooth and elastic, about 5 minutes. Shape the dough into a ball and place in a lightly oiled large bowl, turning to coat the dough with the oil. Cover the bowl with plastic wrap and let the dough rise in a warm spot until tripled in size, 1–1½ hours.

Preheat the oven to 425°F (220°C). Line 2 baking sheets with parchment paper and lightly brush the parchment with oil.

Using well-floured hands, punch down the dough to remove any air bubbles. Turn the dough out onto a lightly floured work surface and shape into a ball, then cut into 8 equal pieces. Roll each piece into a ball. Stick your finger through the center of each ball and gently stretch to create a hole 1–1½ inches (2.5–4 cm) in diameter. Place 4 bagels on each prepared baking sheet and cover loosely with a kitchen towel.

In a large saucepan over high heat, bring the water to a boil, then whisk in the honey. Gently drop 2 or 3 bagels at a time into the boiling water, making sure they have enough room to float without touching. Boil, turning once with a spider or large wooden spoon, for 1 minute per side. Return the boiled bagels to the baking sheets. When the bagels are cool enough to handle, gently reshape them if needed.

Place the everything bagel seasoning in a wide, shallow bowl. Brush the bagels with the egg mixture, covering the surface, sides, and hole. Carefully dip the top of each bagel in the seasoning, pressing down gently to coat. Return the bagels to the baking sheets, spacing them evenly apart.

Bake until the bagels are deep golden brown and sound hollow when gently tapped, rotating the baking sheets between racks halfway through baking, 20–22 minutes.

Transfer the baking sheets to wire racks and let cool for 5 minutes. Transfer the bagels to a wire rack and let cool completely or serve warm with salted butter or cream cheese.

Cinnamon-Raisin Bagels

Bread flour is the secret to creating these dense, chewy bagels. For the most accurate measurement, weigh the flour on a kitchen scale. If you can't find barley malt syrup, use 1 tablespoon light brown sugar instead.

1½ cups (350 ml) warm water (110°F/43°C)

2¾ teaspoons active dry yeast

4 cups (18 oz/508 g) bread flour, plus more for dusting

1 tablespoon barley malt syrup

2½ teaspoons kosher salt

1½ teaspoons pure vanilla extract

1 cup (6 oz/170 g) raisins

3 tablespoons sugar

1 tablespoon ground cinnamon

Canola oil, for greasing

8 cups (1.9 l) water

¼ cup (3 oz/90 g) honey

1 large egg white beaten with 1 tablespoon water

Salted butter or cream cheese, for serving

MAKES 8 BAGELS

In the bowl of a stand mixer, whisk together the warm water and yeast. Let stand until foamy, about 10 minutes. Add the flour, barley malt syrup, salt, and vanilla. Fit the mixer with the dough hook and beat on low speed until just combined, about 2 minutes. Add the raisins, raise the speed to medium, and knead until the dough is sticky and elastic, about 3 minutes.

In a small bowl, whisk together the sugar and cinnamon and sprinkle on a work surface. Scrape the dough out onto the cinnamon-sugar mixture. Using well-floured hands, knead the dough into the mixture until all of it is absorbed, the dough looks swirled, and is smooth and elastic, about 5 minutes. Shape the dough into a ball and place in a lightly oiled large bowl, turning to coat the dough with the oil. Cover the bowl with plastic wrap and let the dough rise in a warm spot until tripled in size, 1–1½ hours.

Preheat the oven to 425°F (220°C). Line 2 baking sheets with parchment paper and lightly brush the parchment with oil.

Using well-floured hands, punch down the dough to remove any air bubbles. Turn the dough out onto a lightly floured work surface and shape into a ball, then cut into 8 equal pieces. Roll each piece into a ball. Stick your finger through the center of each ball and gently stretch to create a hole 1–1½ inches (2.5–4 cm) in diameter. Place 4 bagels on each prepared baking sheet and cover loosely with a kitchen towel.

In a large saucepan over high heat, bring the water to a boil, then whisk in the honey. Gently drop 2 or 3 bagels at a time into the boiling water, making sure they have enough room to float without touching. Boil, turning once with a spider or large wooden spoon, for 1 minute per side. Return the boiled bagels to the baking sheets, spacing them evenly apart. When the bagels are cool enough to handle, gently reshape them if needed. Brush the bagels with the egg mixture, covering the surface, sides, and hole.

Bake until the bagels are deep golden brown and sound hollow when gently tapped, rotating the baking sheets between the racks halfway through baking, 20–22 minutes.

Transfer the baking sheets to wire racks and let cool for 5 minutes. Transfer the bagels to a wire rack and let cool completely or serve warm with salted butter or cream cheese.

Parker House Rolls

Created by Boston's Parker House Hotel in the 1870s, these pull-apart rolls remains a popular dinnertime staple. They are great for soaking up gravy and dunking in soups but they go equally well with just a pat of butter.

1½ cups (350 ml) whole milk

½ cup (4 oz/115 g) unsalted butter, cut into 8 pieces, plus 2 tablespoons unsalted butter, melted and cooled

4½ teaspoons active dry yeast

4 cups (20 oz/625 g) all-purpose flour, plus more for dusting

3 tablespoons sugar

1 tablespoon kosher salt

Canola oil, for greasing

1 tablespoon flaky sea salt

MAKES 24 ROLLS

FOR EVERYTHING VARIATION

1 tablespoon flaky sea salt

1 teaspoon white sesame seeds

½ teaspoon dried onion flakes

½ teaspoon dried garlic flakes

In a small saucepan over medium heat, combine the milk and the ½ cup (4 oz/115 g) butter and heat, whisking occasionally, until the butter melts, about 7 minutes. Remove from the heat and let cool to 105°–115°F (40°–46°C). Add the yeast and stir until dissolved. Let stand until foamy, about 10 minutes.

In the bowl of a stand mixer fitted with the dough hook, beat together the flour, sugar, and kosher salt on low speed until combined, about 30 seconds. Add the yeast mixture and beat until the dough forms a ball, about 1 minute. Raise the speed to medium-low and knead until the dough is smooth and elastic, 4–5 minutes.

Remove the dough from the mixer bowl, oil the inside of the bowl, and return the dough to the bowl, turning to coat the dough with the oil. Cover the bowl tightly with plastic wrap and let the dough rise in a warm spot until doubled in size, about 1 hour.

Grease a 9-by-13-inch (23-by-33-cm) baking dish. Turn the dough out onto a lightly floured work surface and divide the dough in half. Roll out each piece of dough into a log 12 inches (30 cm) long. Using a pastry scraper or a knife, divide each log into 12 equal pieces. Using the cupped palm of your hand, roll and shape each piece into a taut ball.

Transfer the dough balls to the prepared dish, arranging them so there are 4 rows of 6. Cover the dish tightly with plastic wrap and let the dough rise in a warm spot until doubled in size, about 30 minutes.

Preheat the oven to 400°F (200°C).

Remove the plastic wrap from the dish. Brush the rolls with the melted butter and sprinkle with the sea salt.

Bake until the rolls are golden and an instant-read thermometer inserted into the center of a roll registers 190°F (88°C), 18–20 minutes. Invert the rolls onto a wire rack, then turn them right side up onto another rack. Let cool slightly before serving.

EVERYTHING VARIATION

In a small bowl, stir together the sea salt, sesame seeds, onion flakes, and garlic flakes. After brushing the tops of the rolls with the melted butter, sprinkle with the sea salt mixture and bake as directed.

Classic French Brioche

A rich, buttery egg bread, brioche is exceptionally versatile. Spread fresh-baked slices with raspberry jam, then transform leftovers into French toast or bread pudding.

¼ cup (60 ml) warm water (110°F/43°C)

1 tablespoon quick-rise yeast

2¾ cups (12 oz/340 g) all-purpose flour, plus more for dusting

¼ cup (1¼ oz/35 g) nonfat milk powder

3 tablespoons plus 1½ teaspoons sugar

2 teaspoons kosher salt

3 large whole eggs plus 1 large egg, separated

½ cup (4 oz/115 g) plus 3 tablespoons unsalted butter, at room temperature, plus more for serving

Canola oil, for greasing

Leaves from 1 fresh rosemary sprig (optional)

Flaky sea salt, for sprinkling

SERVES 8

In a liquid measuring cup, combine the warm water and yeast. Let stand until foamy, about 10 minutes.

In the bowl of a stand mixer fitted with the dough hook, beat together the flour, milk powder, sugar, and kosher salt on low speed until combined, about 1 minute. Add the yeast mixture, eggs, egg yolk, and butter, raise the speed to medium-low, and knead until the dough is smooth and elastic, about 15 minutes.

Turn the dough out onto a lightly floured work surface and knead gently for 1 minute. Shape the dough into a ball and place in a well-oiled large bowl, turning to coat the dough with the oil. Cover the bowl with a kitchen towel and let the dough rise in a warm spot until doubled in size, about 1½ hours. Remove the towel, cover the bowl with plastic wrap, and refrigerate for at least 6 hours or up to 12 hours. Remove the bowl from the refrigerator and let the dough rise in a warm spot until doubled in size, about 2 hours.

Lightly grease a 9-inch (23-cm) brioche pan. Transfer the dough to the prepared pan, gently reshaping it as needed to fit. Cover the pan with a kitchen towel and let the dough rise in a warm spot until it has risen to just above the top of the pan, about 1 hour.

Preheat the oven to 400°F (200°C).

In a small bowl, lightly beat the remaining egg white. Remove the towel from the pan. Brush the dough with the egg white and sprinkle with the rosemary leaves (if using) and sea salt.

Bake the brioche for 20 minutes, then reduce the oven temperature to 350°F (180°C). Continue to bake until the bread is deep golden brown and an instant-read thermometer inserted into the center registers 165°F (74°C), 25–30 minutes longer. If the bread begins to brown too quickly, cover with aluminum foil.

Transfer the pan to a wire rack and let cool for 10 minutes, then turn the brioche out onto the rack and let cool for 10 minutes longer. Cut into slices and serve warm with butter.

San Francisco Sourdough Bread

This recipe was inspired by the method used at Tartine, a bakery that produces classic San Francisco sourdough bread.

FOR THE STARTER

50 g all-purpose flour

50 g rye flour

100 g room-temperature filtered water (if the room is cold, heat the water to about 80°F/27°C before using)

SERVES 8-10

To save time, you can ask your local bakery if they have a starter you can purchase. They're generally happy to support home bread making! Be sure to ask when it was last fed, so you are able to seamlessly get it on your preferred feeding schedule.

For this recipe, be sure your water does not contain chlorine or chloramine; use bottled water if necessary.

Don't entirely discard your starter after making this bread. Repeat the feeding process once more and then refrigerate until ready to use again. Feed the starter once a week while refrigerated. Remove from the fridge 3 days before baking and feed it on a regular schedule once more and the night before baking your bread. If you are making bread weekly, you can keep you starter at room temperature, feeding it daily and consistently for best results.

There are lots of recipes that incorporate sourdough starter leftovers for added flavor, such as banana bread, focaccia, and waffles.

MAKE THE STARTER (1–2 WEEKS BEFORE MAKING BREAD)

In a quart-size glass jar, bowl, or other container, combine the all-purpose flour, rye flour, and water. Using a small rubber spatula or spoon, mix until no dry bits remain and the mixture resembles thick pancake batter. Cover the top of the container loosely with a lid, kitchen towel, or plastic wrap to prevent the batter from drying out but still allowing it to breathe. You can put a rubber band around the jar to mark the starter's height, so you can see how much it has risen. Let stand at room temperature until the mixture begins to bubble, puff, and lighten in color, 2–3 days. These are all signs of wild yeast activity, which will ultimately become the leaven and add the classic sourdough flavor characteristics to your bread.

DAILY FEED RECIPE

20 g sourdough starter

50 g all-purpose flour

50 g rye flour

100 g room-temperature water
(if the room is cold, heat the
water to about 80°F/27°C
before using)

FEED YOUR STARTER

When your starter begins to show wild yeast activity, begin feeding it regularly at the same time each day. If you feed the starter predictably, it will act predictably, which is what you want when making sourdough. Choose a time that works for your schedule.

A feeding means you are adding flour and water to a portion of the starter, which hosts wild yeast. The flour and water give the wild yeast nutrients to thrive. You will discard a large percentage of it each time, but you can add that to other batters to enhance their flavor.

When the starter falls by about ½ inch (12 mm)—you will see the markings on the glass container— this is an indication that it's time to feed it again. Feeding times will vary depending on your room's temperature. For example, if it's hot outside you may need to feed it twice in one day.

Once your starter begins to act predictably, doubling in size with bubbles and a sour smell and then falling by ½ inch (12 mm), it's ready to use for bread making. This typically occurs after 5–7 days of consistent feeding.

PLAN BEFORE YOU BAKE

Eight to twelve hours before baking, feed your starter to get it ready for making the dough. This step is called "making the leaven." Depending on your feeding schedule, you may need to feed it twice in one day, which is fine. The point is to have your starter in a "mature" stage when you make the dough, i.e., bubbled, lightly doming on top, and sour smelling. We recommend doing this in the morning or at night before bed.

To test if the leaven is mature, gently add about 1 tablespoon of it to a glass of water. If it floats, it's mature and ready to rise your bread.

Continued on page 198

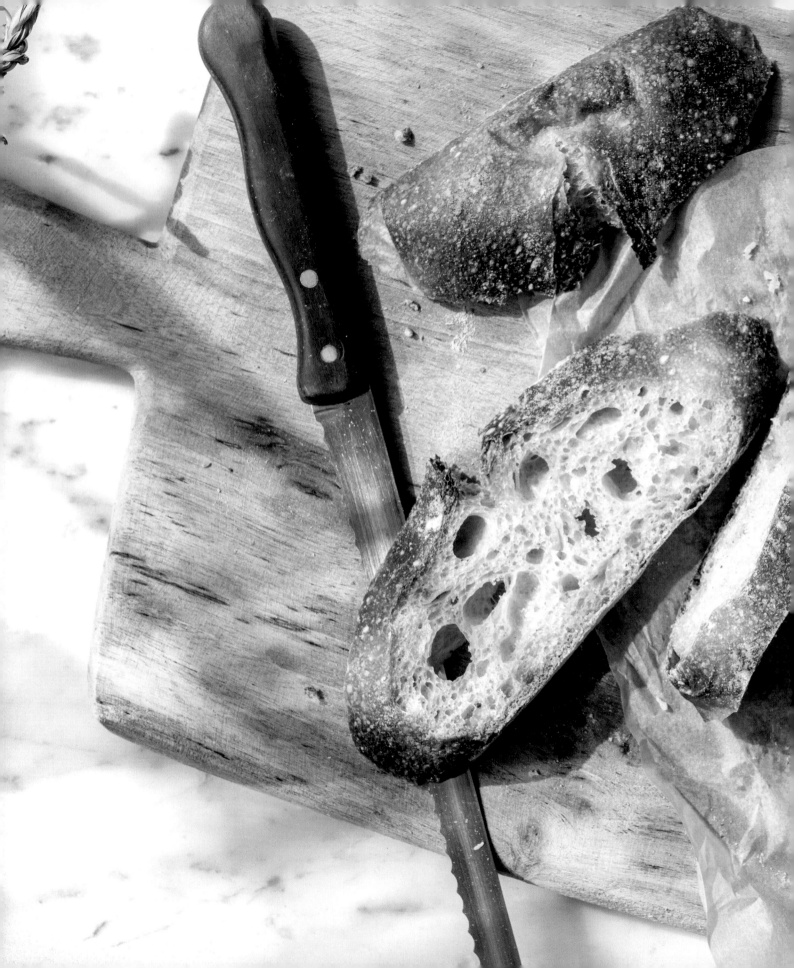

Continued from page 195

FOR THE BREAD

450 g bread flour

50 g whole-wheat flour, plus more for dusting

25 g rye flour

360 g warm water (90°–110°F/32°–43°C)

10 g fine sea salt

100 g leaven (mature sourdough starter)

25 g rice flour for dusting

MAKE THE BREAD

STEP 1: Dough hydration (autolyse)

In a large bowl, whisk together the bread flour, 25 g whole-wheat flour, and the rye flour. Pour 350 g of the warm water and, using a rubber spatula, mix together until no dry bits remain. The dough will look messy and ragged. Cover loosely with a kitchen towel or plastic wrap and let stand at room temperature for 1 hour.

STEP 2: Mix the dough

Uncover the bowl. Using your hands, gently pinch in the salt, leaven (your mature starter), and the remaining 10 g warm water until combined. Pull the bottom of the dough out from underneath and then fold it over on top of itself. Transfer to a clean large bowl. Cover loosely with a kitchen towel or plastic wrap and set in a spot that's 75°–80°F (24°–27°C), ideally in a warm, sunny spot or in a turned-off oven with the light on. If it's colder, it may take longer to rise. Let the dough rest for 30 minutes.

STEP 3: Folds and bulk fermentation

After the dough has rested for 30 minutes, lightly dip your hand in water (this helps with handling the dough) and dramatically pull one underside quadrant of the dough up and over the top of the dough to help build the dough's gluten strength. Repeat for each quadrant. Re-cover the dough and let it rest in a warm spot. Repeat this process every 30 minutes, 4–6 more times (2–3 hours total), until the dough looks 30–50% larger in volume and jiggles, with a slight doming and some visible air bubbles.

STEP 4: Bench pre-shape and rest

When the dough is ready, transfer it to a work surface and lightly dust the dough with whole-wheat flour. Using a bench scraper, gently flip the dough over so the floured side is facing down. Lightly dip your hand in water and pull two of the bottom four corners up and over the dough, sealing them in the middle top of the dough round. Repeat on each side.

Flip the dough over so it is seam side down and cover with a kitchen towel. Let rest at room temperature for 30 minutes.

STEP 5: Prepare the bread basket

While the dough is resting, in a small bowl, whisk together the remaining 25 g whole-wheat flour and rice flour. Use some of the mixture to generously flour a small bread basket (we use an 8-inch/20-cm basket), or line a medium bowl with a kitchen towel and generously flour the towel. Save the remaining flour mixture for Step 8.

STEP 6: Final shaping

Uncover the dough and lightly dust it again with whole-wheat flour. Using a bench scraper, gently flip the dough over so the floured side is facing down. Lightly dip your hand in water and pull two of the bottom four corners up and over the dough, sealing them in the middle top of the dough round. Repeat on each side.

Flip the dough over so it is seam side down. Using your hands and using the surface as an anchor, pull the dough toward you to create a tightly rounded shape. Shift the dough and pull toward you again. This will help mold the dough into a smooth, tight round.

STEP 7: Final proof

Using the bench scraper, gently flip the dough round over so it is seam side up and transfer to the floured bread basket or towel-lined bowl, keeping the seam side up. Cover with a kitchen towel or plastic wrap and let the dough rest in the same warm spot, ideally 75°–80°F (24°–27°C) for 3–4 hours. If it's colder, it will be 5–6 hours; if warmer, 2–3 hours. You can also let the dough rest in its bowl in the refrigerator, with the dough wrapped with plastic wrap to prevent condensation, for 10–12 hours, which will help it develop more flavor. Bring to room temperature before baking.

To check if your dough is ready to bake, gently press it with your finger; it should slowly spring back and there should be a barely perceptible depression, but not much. If it quickly springs back, give it more time. If it leaves a depression, the dough may be overproofed.

STEP 8: Score and bake

About 30 minutes before your bread is ready, place a lidded Dutch oven in a cold oven and preheat the oven to 500°F (260°C). When your oven is heated and the dough is ready, lightly dust the exposed side of the dough with the reserved whole-wheat flour mixture. Line a small cutting board with parchment paper and place it, parchment side down, on your bread basket. Quickly flip the bread over onto the parchment.

Carefully but quickly remove the Dutch oven from the oven and remove the lid. Grab the corners of the parchment and transfer the dough, still on the parchment, to the pot. Using a sharp knife or blade, quickly score the top of the bread; we like to score an "X" or a slash "/" with a slight curve to it, which will allow the bread to rise and expand. The Dutch oven will be hot, so take care during this step.

Replace the lid and return the pot in the oven. Reduce the oven temperature to 450°F (230°C) and bake for 20 minutes. Remove the lid and bake uncovered until the bread is dark golden, 20–25 minutes longer.

Transfer the bread from the Dutch oven to a cooling rack, and test for doneness by lightly tapping the bottom of your loaf—it should sound hollow. Let cool for at least 1 hour before serving. This is important for the bread baking, as the proteins will continue to cook as the loaf cools.

Gluten-Free Skillet Corn Bread with Thyme & Honey

Be sure to check whether your cornmeal is fine-, medium-, or coarse-ground. Coarse-ground cornmeal, while lending an intense corn flavor, cannot be substituted for fine- or medium-ground as the bake time will vary substantially.

2 cups (14 oz/440 g) gluten-free coarse-ground cornmeal

¼ cup (1¾ oz/50 g) sugar

1½ teaspoons kosher salt

½ teaspoon baking powder

½ teaspoon baking soda

1½ cups (350 ml) buttermilk

1 large egg

4 tablespoons (2 oz/60 g) unsalted butter, melted and cooled, plus 6 tablespoons (3 oz/90 g) unsalted butter, at room temperature

Wildflower honey

1 tablespoon chopped fresh thyme

Flaky sea salt, for sprinkling

SERVES 8-10

Place a 10-inch (25-cm) cast-iron frying pan in the oven and preheat the oven to 450°F (230°C).

In a large bowl, whisk together the cornmeal, sugar, kosher salt, baking powder, and baking soda. In a medium bowl, whisk together the buttermilk and egg. Add the egg mixture to the cornmeal mixture and stir until combined. Stir in the melted butter.

Carefully remove the pan from the oven and add 1 tablespoon of the room-temperature butter, swirling the pan until the butter is melted and coats the pan. Scrape the batter into the pan and spread evenly. The batter should immediately begin to sizzle around the edges.

Bake until the corn bread is golden brown and a toothpick inserted into the center of the bread comes out clean, about 12 minutes.

Transfer the pan to a wire rack and spread the remaining 5 tablespoons (2½ oz/70 g) butter over the corn bread. Liberally drizzle with honey, and sprinkle with the thyme and sea salt. Let cool for 15 minutes, then cut into slices and serve.

Buttermilk Biscuits with Herbed Butter & Honey

Master these tender, fluffy biscuits and you'll have a go-to side for any dinner. When cutting the dough, press straight down and back up with the cutter without twisting it—twisting the cutter crimps the dough's edges, resulting in flat biscuits. Serve drizzled with herbed butter and honey.

FOR THE BISCUITS

2 cups (9 oz/250 g) all-purpose flour, plus more for dusting

1½ teaspoons kosher salt

1½ teaspoons baking powder

½ teaspoon baking soda

½ cup (4 oz/115 g) cold unsalted butter, cut into ½-inch (12-mm) pieces

½ cup (120 ml) cold buttermilk

½ cup (120 ml) cold heavy cream

FOR THE HERBED BUTTER

½ cup (4 oz/115 g) unsalted butter, at room temperature

1 tablespoon finely minced fresh rosemary

2 teaspoons finely minced fresh thyme

Kosher salt and freshly ground pepper

Honey, for serving

MAKES 8 BISCUITS

To make the biscuits, preheat the oven to 375°F (190°C). Line a baking sheet with parchment paper.

In a large bowl, whisk together the flour, salt, baking powder, and baking soda. Add the butter and toss to coat with the flour mixture. Using a pastry blender or 2 knives and working quickly, cut in the butter until pea-size pieces form. Add the buttermilk and cream and stir until a wet, shaggy dough forms.

Turn the dough out onto a well-floured work surface and dust the top of the dough with flour. Using floured hands, knead once or twice until the dough comes together, then pat into a round about 1 inch (2.5 cm) thick. Dip a 2-inch (5-cm) round cutter in flour and cut out as many biscuits as possible, taking care not to twist the cutter but instead pressing straight down and lifting straight up. Transfer the biscuits to the prepared baking sheet, spacing them about 1 inch (2.5 cm) apart. Gather up the dough scraps, pat out again, and cut out more biscuits.

Bake until the biscuits have risen and are golden brown, about 20 minutes. Transfer the biscuits to a wire rack and let cool for about 5 minutes.

Meanwhile, make the herbed butter: In a small bowl, stir together the butter, rosemary, and thyme, and season with salt and pepper. Serve the biscuits warm with the herbed butter and honey.

Classic Focaccia

A loaf of focaccia, with its crunchy crust and fluffy interior, can stand on its own at your dinner table, but feel free to accompany it with pesto or herbed olive oil for dipping to enhance the bread's flavor.

6¼ cups (1 lb 9 oz/710 g) bread flour

2½ cups (600 ml) room-temperature water (70°–74°F/21°–23°C)

3 teaspoons sugar

½ cup (120 ml) warm water (95°F/35°C)

1 package (2¼ teaspoons) active dry yeast

1 tablespoon plus 1½ teaspoons kosher salt

½ cup (120 ml) extra-virgin olive oil, plus more as needed

Flaky sea salt, for sprinkling

MAKES ONE 18-BY-13-INCH (45-BY-33-CM) RECTANGLE; SERVES 8

In the bowl of a stand mixer fitted with the dough hook, beat together the flour, room-temperature water, and 1½ teaspoons of the sugar on low speed until a shaggy dough forms, 2–3 minutes. Cover the bowl with a kitchen towel and let stand while you prepare the yeast mixture.

In a small bowl, whisk together the warm water, yeast, and remaining 1½ teaspoons sugar. Let stand until foamy, about 5–10 minutes.

Remove the towel from the mixer bowl. With the mixer on low speed, add the yeast mixture a little at a time and beat until the liquid is absorbed, 1–2 minutes. If necessary, stop the mixer, remove the bowl, and knead any remaining water into the dough by hand. Add the kosher salt, raise the speed to medium, and beat until the dough is very elastic and sticky, and pulls away from the sides of the bowl, 3–5 minutes.

Coat the inside of a large bowl with 3 tablespoons of the oil. Scrape the dough into the bowl, turning to coat the dough with the oil. Cover the bowl loosely with plastic wrap and let the dough rise in a warm spot until doubled in size, about 2½ hours.

Coat a rimmed baking sheet with 2 tablespoons of the oil.

Fold the dough over itself twice in the bowl to deflate slightly. Transfer the dough to the prepared baking sheet. Using oiled hands, gently stretch the dough out to the edges and corners of the pan. If the dough springs back toward the center, cover with plastic wrap and let stand for 10 minutes, then repeat to stretch the dough. Cover the pan with oiled plastic wrap and refrigerate for at least 2 hours or up to overnight.

Remove the focaccia from the refrigerator and let stand in a warm spot 1 hour before baking, until the dough has risen to the top of the pan.

Preheat the oven to 450°F (230°C).

Remove the plastic wrap from the pan and drizzle 2 tablespoons of the oil over the dough, gently distributing it as evenly as possible. Using oiled fingers, press your fingertips firmly into the dough to make deep dimples over the entire surface. Sprinkle generously with sea salt.

Bake until the focaccia is deep golden brown all over, 20–25 minutes; halfway through baking, drizzle all over the dough with about 1 tablespoon oil to help the crust brown.

Transfer the baking sheet to a wire rack and let cool for 10 minutes. Drizzle the focaccia with more oil and sprinkle with more sea salt. Cut into slices and serve warm or at room temperature.

Focaccia with Caramelized Onions & Herbs

The caramelized onions ensure that this focaccia stays wonderfully moist. The bread will keep for about 3 days stored in an airtight container at room temperature. If you don't have avocado oil on hand for cooking the onions, substitute another oil with a high burning point, such as canola, sunflower, or peanut oil.

Focaccia dough (page 203)

2 tablespoons avocado oil or unsalted butter

2 yellow onions, halved lengthwise, then thinly sliced lengthwise

Flaky sea salt, for sprinkling

4 tablespoons olive oil, plus more for drizzling

3 cloves garlic, thinly sliced

Leaves from 1 fresh rosemary sprig

Fresh basil leaves, oregano, rosemary, or other herbs, for garnish

MAKES ONE 18-BY-13-INCH (45-BY-33-CM) RECTANGLE; SERVES 8

Make the focaccia dough as directed, refrigerating the dough on the rimmed baking sheet for 2 hours or up to overnight.

Meanwhile, make the caramelized onions and rosemary-garlic oil (you can do this a few days ahead). In a large frying pan over medium heat, warm the avocado oil or melt the butter until sizzling. Add the onions and a pinch of kosher salt and cook, stirring frequently, until translucent, about 5–10 minutes. Reduce the heat to medium-low and cook, stirring every few minutes, until the onions are dark brown and caramelized, about 40 minutes. Occasionally deglaze the pan with ¼ cup (60 ml) water, stirring to scrape up the browned bits. Transfer the onions to a bowl and set aside.

While the onions are caramelizing, in a small frying pan over low heat, warm 2 tablespoons of the olive oil. Add the garlic and rosemary and cook, stirring occasionally, until fragrant, 1–2 minutes. Remove from the heat and let cool.

Remove the focaccia from the refrigerator and let stand in a warm spot 1 hour before baking, until the dough has risen to the top of the pan.

Preheat the oven to 450°F (230°C).

Remove the plastic wrap from the pan. Stir 1 tablespoon more olive oil into the rosemary-garlic oil and drizzle over the dough, gently distributing it as evenly as possible. Using oiled fingers, press your fingertips firmly into the dough to make deep dimples over the entire surface. Arrange the caramelized onions on top. Sprinkle generously with sea salt.

Bake until the focaccia is deep golden brown all over, 20–25 minutes; halfway through baking, drizzle all over the dough with about 1 tablespoon olive oil to help the crust brown nicely.

Transfer the baking sheet to a wire rack and let cool for 10 minutes. Drizzle the focaccia with more olive oil, sprinkle with more sea salt, and garnish with herbs. Cut into slices and serve warm or at room temperature.

Focaccia with Cherries, Honey & Thyme

Serve this cherry-topped loaf alongside your favorite summer salad and you'll enjoy a memorable meal. Slathering it with some mascarpone cheese makes for an excellent segway into a dessert course.

Focaccia dough (page 203)

3 tablespoons olive oil

½ pound (225 g) fresh or thawed frozen cherries, pitted

Flaky sea salt, for sprinkling

Honey, for drizzling

Fresh thyme sprigs and leaves, for garnish

Makes one 18-by-13-inch (45-by-33-cm) rectangle; **SERVES 8**

Make the focaccia dough as directed, refrigerating the dough on the rimmed baking sheet for 2 hours or up to overnight.

Remove the focaccia from the refrigerator and let stand in a warm spot 1 hour before baking, until the dough has risen to the top of the pan.

Preheat the oven to 450°F (230°C).

Remove the plastic wrap from the pan and drizzle 2 tablespoons of the oil over the dough. Using oiled fingers, press your fingertips firmly into the dough to make deep dimples over the entire surface. Arrange the cherries on top, alternating them with the dimples and pressing the cherries down slightly into the dough. Sprinkle generously with sea salt.

Bake until the focaccia is deep golden brown all over and the cherries have collapsed slightly, 20–25 minutes; halfway through baking, drizzle all over the dough with about 1 tablespoon oil to help the crust brown nicely.

Transfer the baking sheet to a wire rack and let cool for 10 minutes. Drizzle the focaccia with honey, sprinkle with more sea salt, and garnish with thyme sprigs and leaves. Cut into slices and serve warm or at room temperature.

BASICS

SUGAR COOKIES

In a bowl, sift together the flour, baking powder, and salt. Set aside.

In the bowl of a stand mixer fitted with the paddle attachment, beat together the butter and sugar on medium speed until light and fluffy, about 3 minutes. Reduce the speed to low and add the egg yolks one at a time, beating well after each addition. Add the vanilla and beat until combined, about 1 minute. Stop the mixer and scrape down the sides of the bowl. Add the flour mixture and beat on low speed until combined, about 1 minute.

Turn the dough out onto a work surface, divide into 2 equal pieces, and shape each into a disk. Wrap separately in plastic wrap and refrigerate for at least 1 hour or up to overnight. Let the dough soften slightly at room temperature before continuing.

Preheat the oven to 350°F (180°C). Line a baking sheet with parchment paper.

On a lightly floured work surface, roll out 1 dough disk ¼ inch (6 mm) thick. Using cookie cutters, cut out the desired shapes. Transfer the cookies to the prepared baking sheet, spacing them about 1½ inches (4 cm) apart. Repeat with the remaining dough disk. Gather up the scraps of dough, reroll, and cut out more cookies.

Bake until the cookies are golden on the edges, about 8 minutes. Transfer the cookies to a wire rack and let cool completely.

MAKES ABOUT 2 DOZEN COOKIES

2½ cups (12½ oz/390 g) all-purpose flour, plus more for dusting

1 teaspoon baking powder

½ teaspoon kosher salt

1 cup (8 oz/250 g) unsalted butter, at room temperature

¾ cup (6 oz/185 g) sugar

3 large egg yolks

1½ teaspoons pure vanilla extract

ROYAL ICING

In a large bowl, combine the confectioners' sugar, meringue powder, ½ cup (125 ml) warm water, and extract (if using). Using an electric mixer on medium speed, beat until the mixture is fluffy yet dense, 7–8 minutes. To thin the icing, use a silicone spatula to stir in more warm water, 1 teaspoon at a time. To test the consistency, drizzle a spoonful of icing into the bowl; a ribbon should remain on the surface for about 5 seconds. Cover and refrigerate airtight for up to 1 week. Stir vigorously just before using.

MAKES ABOUT 3 CUPS (24 FL OZ/750 ML)

4 cups (1 lb/500 g) confectioners' sugar

3 tablespoons meringue powder

½ teaspoon extract, such as vanilla or almond (optional)

BASIC PIE DOUGH

To make the dough by hand, in a large bowl, stir together the flour, sugar, and salt. Using a pastry blender or 2 knives, cut in the butter until the texture resembles coarse cornmeal, with butter pieces no larger than small peas. Add the water and mix with a fork just until the dough comes together.

To make the dough in a food processor, combine the flour, sugar, and salt in the processor and pulse 2 or 3 times to mix evenly. Add the butter and pulse 8–10 times, until the butter pieces are the size of small peas. Add the water and pulse 10–12 times. Stop the machine and squeeze a piece of dough. If it crumbles, add more of the water, 1 tablespoon at a time, and pulse just until the dough holds together when pinched.

Transfer the dough to a work surface and shape into a disk. Refrigerate for 30 minutes.

Lightly flour the work surface, then flatten the disk with 6–8 gentle taps of the rolling pin. Lift the dough and give it a quarter turn. Lightly dust the top of the dough or the rolling pin with flour as needed, then roll out into a round at least 12 inches (30 cm) in diameter and about ⅛ inch (3 mm) thick.

MAKES ONE 9-INCH (23-CM) CRUST

1¼ cups (6½ oz/200 g) all-purpose flour, plus more for dusting

1 tablespoon sugar

¼ teaspoon kosher salt

½ cup (4 oz/125 g) cold unsalted butter, cut into ¼-inch (6-mm) cubes

3 tablespoons very cold water, plus more as needed

GLUTEN-FREE PIE DOUGH

In a food processor, combine the almond flour, potato starch, flour, sugar, and salt and pulse 2 or 3 times to mix evenly. Add the butter and pulse until the texture resembles coarse cornmeal, with butter pieces no larger than small peas. Add the egg and process on low speed until the dough just comes together. Transfer the dough to a work surface and shape into a disk. Wrap well in plastic wrap and refrigerate for at least 1 hour or up to 2 days.

When ready to use, substitute this dough into any recipe that uses the Basic Pie Dough to make it gluten-free.

MAKES ONE 9-INCH (23-CM) CRUST

⅔ cup (3 oz/90 g) almond flour

⅓ cup (1 oz/40 g) potato starch

⅓ cup (2 oz/60 g) gluten-free all-purpose flour

1 tablespoon confectioners' sugar

½ teaspoon kosher salt

½ cup (4 oz/125 g) cold unsalted butter, cut into cubes

1 large egg

CHOCOLATE PIE DOUGH

To make the dough by hand, in a large bowl, stir together the flour, cocoa powder, brown sugar, espresso powder, and salt. Using a pastry blender or 2 knives, cut in the butter until the texture resembles coarse cornmeal, with butter pieces no larger than small peas. Add the coffee and mix with a fork just until the dough comes together.

To make the dough in a food processor, combine the flour, cocoa powder, brown sugar, espresso powder, and salt in the processor and pulse 2 or 3 times to mix evenly. Add the butter and pulse 8–10 times, until the butter pieces are the size of small peas. Add the coffee and pulse 10–12 times. Stop the machine and squeeze a piece of dough. If it crumbles, add more of the coffee, 1 tablespoon at a time, and pulse just until the dough holds together when pinched.

Transfer the dough to a work surface and shape into a disk. Refrigerate for 30 minutes.

Lightly flour the work surface, then flatten the disk with 6–8 gentle taps of the rolling pin. Lift the dough and give it a quarter turn. Lightly dust the top of the dough or the rolling pin with flour as needed, then roll out into a round at least 12 inches (30 cm) in diameter and about ⅛ inch (3 mm) thick.

MAKES ONE 9-INCH (23-CM) CRUST

1¼ cups (6½ oz/200 g) all-purpose flour, plus more for dusting

1 cup (3 oz/90 g) unsweetened cocoa powder

1 tablespoon firmly packed light brown sugar

1 teaspoon espresso powder

¼ teaspoon kosher salt

½ cup (4 oz/125 g) cold unsalted butter, cut into ¼-inch (6-mm) cubes

3 tablespoons cold coffee, plus more as needed

SHORTBREAD CRUST

Preheat the oven to 375°F (190°C).

In the bowl of a stand mixer fitted with the paddle attachment, beat together the butter, granulated sugar, and brown sugar on medium speed until light and fluffy, about 3 minutes. Add the egg yolks, flour, salt, and vanilla and beat until just combined, about 2 minutes.

Transfer the dough to a 9-inch (23-cm) pie dish and spread evenly across the bottom and up the sides, pressing until compact. Pierce the bottom of the crust all over with a fork and freeze for 20 minutes.

Line the crust with aluminum foil and fill with pie weights. Bake until lightly browned, about 20 minutes. Remove the foil and weights. Let cool completely on a wire rack before filling.

MAKES ONE 9-INCH (23-CM) CRUST

6 tablespoons (3 oz/90 g) unsalted butter, at room temperature

3 tablespoons granulated sugar

3 tablespoons firmly packed light brown sugar

2 large egg yolks

1¼ cups (6½ oz/200 g) all-purpose flour

1 teaspoon kosher salt

1 teaspoon pure vanilla extract

WAFER COOKIE CRUST

Preheat the oven to 350°F (180°C).

In a food processor, pulse the cookies until fine crumbs form. Add the sugar and salt and pulse a few times to mix evenly. Add the melted butter and pulse until the texture resembles wet sand. Gently press the mixture evenly into the bottom and up the sides of a 9-inch (23-cm) pie dish, pressing until compact.

Bake until the crust is golden brown, about 10 minutes. Let cool completely on a wire rack before filling.

MAKES ONE 9-INCH (23-CM) CRUST

4½ cups (9 oz/280 g) vanilla or chocolate wafer cookies

1 tablespoon sugar

1 teaspoon kosher salt

½ cup (4 oz/125 g) unsalted butter, melted and cooled

PRETZEL CRUST

Preheat the oven to 350°F (180°C).

In a food processor, pulse the pretzels until finely ground. Add the brown sugar, melted butter, and salt and pulse until the texture resembles wet sand. Gently press the mixture evenly into the bottom and up the sides of a 9½-inch (24-cm) pie dish, pressing until compact.

Bake until the crust is golden brown, about 10 minutes. Let cool completely on a wire rack before filling.

MAKES ONE 9-INCH (23-CM) CRUST

4½ cups (6½ oz/200 g) pretzels

1 tablespoon firmly packed light brown sugar

½ cup (4 oz/125 g) unsalted butter, melted and cooled

Pinch of kosher salt

CORN BREAD TOPPING

In a medium bowl, whisk together the cornmeal, flour, sugar, baking powder, and salt. In a large bowl, whisk together the egg and buttermilk. Add the cornmeal mixture to the egg mixture and stir until just combined. Fold in the melted butter.

Scoop the dough on top of the filling to cover.

MAKES ENOUGH TO TOP 6-8 COCOTTES OR RAMEKINS

1 cup (5 oz/155 g) cornmeal

1 cup (5 oz/155 g) all-purpose flour

2 tablespoons sugar

1 tablespoon baking powder

1 teaspoon kosher salt

1 large egg

1 cup (250 ml) buttermilk

4 tablespoons (2 oz/60 g) unsalted butter, melted and cooled

FILO DOUGH TOP

Remove the filo sheets from their package and place the stacks of sheets flat on a work surface. Cut the stack crosswise in half; rewrap one half and reserve for another use.

Place 1 sheet of filo flat on the work surface; keep the remaining sheets lightly covered with a damp paper towel to prevent drying. Place a second sheet rotated at a slight angle on top of the first and brush lightly with butter. Repeat with the remaining sheets, rotating each one slightly and brushing with butter, to form a rough round that is stacked in the center.

MAKES 1 FILO DOUGH TOP

1 box (1 lb/500g) thawed frozen filo dough

½ cup (4 oz/125 g) unsalted butter, melted

CREAM CHEESE DOUGH

In a food processor, combine the flour, salt, and butter and process until the texture resembles coarse cornmeal, with butter pieces no larger than small peas. Add the cream cheese and pulse a few times, just until the dough comes together. Transfer the dough to a work surface and shape into a disk. Wrap well in plastic wrap and refrigerate for 30 minutes.

MAKES ONE 9-INCH (23-CM) CRUST

2 cups (10 oz/315 g) all-purpose flour

1 teaspoon kosher salt

1 cup (8 oz/250 g) cold unsalted butter, cut into cubes

½ lb (250 g) cream cheese, at room temperature

HERBED BISCUIT DOUGH

In a food processor, combine the flour, salt, baking powder, baking soda, and butter and pulse until the texture resembles coarse cornmeal, with butter pieces no larger than small peas. Add the buttermilk, thyme, and rosemary and pulse until combined.

Cover the filling with the dough.

MAKES ENOUGH TO TOP A 9-BY-13-INCH (23-BY-33-CM) BAKING DISH

1 cup (5 oz/155 g) all-purpose flour

1 teaspoon salt

1 teaspoon baking powder

½ teaspoon baking soda

4 tablespoons (2 oz/60 g) cold unsalted butter, cut into cubes

⅔ cup (160 ml) buttermilk

1 tablespoon chopped fresh thyme

1 tablespoon chopped fresh rosemary

WEEKEND PIZZA DOUGH

In the bowl of a stand mixer, whisk together the warm water, yeast, and sugar. Let stand until foamy, 5–10 minutes. Add the flour and salt and beat on low speed until just combined. Fit the mixer with the dough hook, slowly drizzle in the oil, raise the speed to medium, and knead until the dough is very elastic, sticky, and pulls away from the sides of the bowl, about 5 minutes.

If the dough has not already formed a ball, shape it into a ball and place in a lightly oiled large bowl, turning to coat the dough with the oil. Cover the bowl loosely with plastic wrap and let the dough rise in a warm spot until doubled in size, about 1 hour.

Turn the dough out onto a lightly floured work surface and knead into a ball. If the dough is too sticky to handle, knead in up to ½ cup (2 oz/60 g) more flour. For a thinner, crisper crust, divide the dough in half and knead into 2 balls after adding the flour. Transfer the dough to a clean large bowl, or 2 bowls if you divided the dough, and cover tightly with plastic wrap. Refrigerate for 3–6 hours.

Place a pizza stone or a large cast-iron frying pan in the oven. Preheat the oven to 500°F (260°C) for 1 hour. Remove the dough from the refrigerator and let stand at room temperature for 30–45 minutes.

On a floured surface, using your hands, shape the dough into a round about 10 inches wide, then tuck the dough under itself and form a tight ball. Using your fingertips, punch the center of the dough down, repeating in circular motions, and moving outward toward the edges but making sure to not punch down the edges of the dough. Then, using your hands, shape and gently stretch the dough into a 10-inch pizza crust. When the dough is the size and shape you like, transfer to a floured pizza peel or inverted baking sheet. Gently press down on the center of the dough and repeat this motion outward, leaving ½–1 inch (12 mm–2.5 cm) of the dough edges untouched (this will become the edges of the crust).

Arrange the toppings on the dough and carefully slide the pizza from the peel onto the preheated stone. If using a cast-iron frying pan, remove the pan from the oven and carefully slide the pizza onto the pan. Bake until the crust is browned underneath, 10–12 minutes. Remove from the oven, cut into slices, and serve right away.

MAKES 1 OR 2 PIZZAS

1 cup (240 ml) warm water (90°–110°F/32°–43°C)

1 package (2¼ teaspoons) active dry yeast

1 teaspoon sugar

2½ cups (11 oz/310 g) all-purpose flour, plus more as needed

1½ teaspoons kosher salt

2 tablespoons extra-virgin olive oil, plus more as needed

Pizza toppings as desired

WHITE CAKE

Preheat the oven to 350°F (180°C). Grease two 8-inch (20-cm) round cake pans, line the bottoms of the pans with parchment paper, then grease the parchment. Dust with flour, then tap out any excess.

In a bowl, sift together the flour, baking powder, baking soda, and salt. Set aside. In the bowl of a stand mixer fitted with the whisk attachment, beat together the egg whites and 1 cup (8 oz/250 g) of the sugar on medium-high speed until soft peaks form, about 4 minutes. Set aside.

In the clean bowl of the stand mixer fitted with the paddle attachment, beat together the butter and the remaining 1 cup (8 oz/250 g) sugar on medium speed until light and fluffy, about 2 minutes. Add the egg and vanilla and beat until combined, about 1 minute. Stop the mixer and scrape down the sides of the bowl. With the mixer on low speed, add the flour mixture in 3 additions, alternating with the buttermilk and beginning and ending with the flour, and beat until combined. Stop the mixer and scrape down the sides of the bowl. Raise the speed to high and beat for 20 seconds.

Using a rubber spatula, gently fold the egg whites into the butter mixture until completely incorporated, taking care not to deflate the peaks. Divide the batter evenly between the prepared pans and spread evenly. Bake until a toothpick inserted into the center of the cakes comes out clean, 40–45 minutes. Transfer the pans to wire racks and let cool for 10 minutes, then invert the cakes onto the racks and let cool completely. The cakes can be stored in an airtight container at room temperature for up to 2 days.

VARIATION
Champagne Cake: Make the white cake batter, replacing the 1½ cups (375 ml) buttermilk with ¾ cup (180 ml) buttermilk and ¾ cup (180 ml) sparkling wine.

MAKES TWO TO FOUR ROUND CAKE LAYERS, ONE 9-BY-13-INCH (23-BY-33-CM) SHEET CAKE, OR 24 CUPCAKES

¾ cup (6 oz/185 g) unsalted butter, at room temperature, plus more for greasing

2¾ cups (14 oz/440 g) all-purpose flour, plus more for dusting

2½ teaspoons baking powder

¾ teaspoon baking soda

¾ teaspoon kosher salt

3 large egg whites plus 1 large egg

2 cups (1 lb/500 g) sugar

1 tablespoon pure vanilla extract

1½ cups (375 ml) buttermilk

YELLOW CAKE

Preheat the oven to 350°F (180°C). Grease two 8-inch (20-cm) round cake pans, line the bottoms of the pans with parchment paper, then grease the parchment. Dust with flour, then tap out any excess.

In a bowl, sift together the flour, baking powder, baking soda, and salt. Set aside.

In the bowl of a stand mixer fitted with the paddle attachment, beat together the butter and sugar on medium speed until light and fluffy, about 2 minutes. Add the eggs one at a time, and then the egg yolks and vanilla and beat until incorporated. Stop the mixer and scrape down the sides of the bowl. With the mixer on low speed, add the flour mixture in 3 additions, alternating with the buttermilk and beginning and ending with the flour and beat until combined. Stop the mixture and scrape down the sides of the bowl. Raise the speed to high and beat for 20 seconds.

Divide the batter evenly between the prepared pans and spread evenly. Bake until a toothpick inserted into the center of the cakes comes out clean, about 55 minutes. Transfer the pans to wire racks and let cool for 10 minutes, then invert the cakes onto the racks and let cool completely. The cakes can be stored in an airtight container at room temperature for up to 2 days.

MAKES TWO 8-INCH (20-CM) ROUND CAKES, ONE 10-INCH (25-CM) BUNDT CAKE, OR ONE 9-BY-13-INCH (23-BY-33-CM) SHEET CAKE

1 cup (8 oz/250 g) unsalted butter, at room temperature, plus more for greasing

3 cups (15 oz/470 g) all-purpose flour, plus more for dusting

2 teaspoons baking powder

¾ teaspoon baking soda

¾ teaspoon kosher salt

2 cups (1 lb/500 g) sugar

2 large eggs plus 2 large egg yolks

1 tablespoon pure vanilla extract

2 cups (500 ml) buttermilk

RASPBERRY FILLING

In a saucepan over medium-high heat, combine the raspberries, sugar, lemon zest and juice, and cornstarch and bring to a simmer. Cook, stirring occasionally, until just beginning to thicken, about 2 minutes. Reduce the heat to low and cook, stirring occasionally, until the mixture is bubbling and thick enough to coat the back of a spoon, about 3 minutes. Transfer to a bowl and let cool completely. Store in an airtight container in the refrigerator for up to 1 week.

MAKES ABOUT 1 CUP (10 OZ/315 G)

3 cups (12 oz/375 g) frozen raspberries

⅓ cup (3 oz/90 g) sugar

2 teaspoons grated lemon zest

2 tablespoons fresh lemon juice

1 tablespoon cornstarch

LEMON CURD

In a saucepan over medium heat, combine the egg yolks, sugar, and lemon zest and juice. Cook, whisking often, until the mixture is thick enough to coat the back of a spoon, about 10 minutes. Add the butter and cook, stirring often, until melted, about 3 minutes. Reduce the heat to low and cook, whisking constantly, until it starts to thicken, about 1 minute longer. Strain the lemon curd through a fine-mesh sieve into a bowl. Cover and refrigerate for at least 2 hours or up to 3 days.

VARIATION

To make lime curd, substitute an equal amount of lime zest and juice for the lemon.

MAKES 1 CUP (250 ML)

8 large egg yolks

1½ cups (6 oz/180 g) sugar

2 tablespoons grated lemon zest

¾ cup (180 ml) fresh lemon juice

¾ cup (6 oz/180 g) cold unsalted butter, cut into pieces

MARZIPAN

In a food processor, combine the almond flour and confectioners' sugar and pulse until well combined. Add the extract, rose water (if using), and egg white and pulse until a thick dough forms. If the dough is wet and sticky to the touch, add 1–2 tablespoons more almond flour and pulse again. Add food coloring, if using, and pulse until evenly blended. If using more than one color, divide the dough into batches and dye separately. Turn the dough out onto a work surface and knead a few times. Shape into a disk, wrap in plastic wrap, and refrigerate for at least 1 hour or up to 1 month.

Let the dough stand at room temperature for about 5 minutes. Roll out the dough ¼ inch (6 mm) thick. If your rolling pin sticks to the dough, coat the pin very lightly with confectioners' sugar. Using a knife, cookie cutter, or pastry cutter, cut out the desired shapes and use right away.

MAKES ABOUT ¾ LB (375 G)

1½ cups (5 oz/120 g) super-fine almond flour, plus more as needed

1½ cups (6 oz/185 g) confectioners' sugar, plus more as needed

2 teaspoons almond or pure vanilla extract

1 teaspoon rose water (optional)

1 large egg white

Food coloring as desired (optional)

AMARETTO-POACHED PEARS

In a large saucepan over medium heat, combine the amaretto, brown sugar, lemon zest and juice, and cinnamon stick and bring to a simmer, whisking to dissolve the sugar. Add the pears and simmer, turning them over every 10 minutes if not completely submerged, until tender when pierced with a knife, about 1 hour. Let cool completely in the liquid, then remove from the liquid, reserving it if desired. Cut the pears lengthwise into slices about ½ inch (12 mm) thick or leave the halves whole.

The pears can be refrigerated in the poaching liquid for up to 1 week; they will become more flavorful as they soak in the liquid.

MAKES ENOUGH TO TOP ONE ROUND LAYER CAKE

1½ cups (375 ml) amaretto

2 tablespoons firmly packed light brown sugar

2-inch (5-cm) strip lemon zest

Juice of 1 lemon

1 cinnamon stick

3 d'Anjou pears, peeled, halved, and cored

VANILLA BUTTERCREAM

Combine the egg whites and sugar in the bowl of a heatproof stand mixer and set over but not touching barely simmering water in a large saucepan. Cook, whisking constantly, until the mixture is hot to the touch, about 160°F (71°C).

Attach the bowl to the stand mixer fitted with the whisk attachment, add the vanilla, and beat on medium-high speed until the mixture reaches room temperature, about 15 minutes. Switch to the paddle attachment, add the butter a few tablespoons at a time, and beat on low speed until incorporated. If the buttercream becomes grainy, raise the speed to high and beat until smooth, about 1 minute.

MAKES ENOUGH FOR ONE ROUND LAYER CAKE OR 12 MINI LAYER CAKES

3 large egg whites

1 cup (8 oz/250 g) sugar

1 teaspoon pure vanilla extract

1 cup (8 oz/250 g) unsalted butter, at room temperature

CHOCOLATE FROSTING

Put the chocolate chips in the bowl of a stand mixer. Set aside. In a saucepan over medium-low heat, bring the cream to a simmer, about 3 minutes. Pour the hot cream over the chocolate and let stand for 10 minutes. Using a handheld whisk, whisk until the mixture is velvety and smooth and completely cooled.

Attach the bowl to the stand mixer fitted with the whisk attachment and beat on high speed until the frosting is light and fluffy, about 3 minutes. If it is too thick, beat in 1 tablespoon cream at a time until the desired consistency is reached.

MAKES ENOUGH FOR ONE ROUND LAYER CAKE

3 cups (18 oz/560 g) semisweet chocolate chips

3 cups (750 ml) heavy cream, plus more as needed

COCONUT BUTTERCREAM

In the bowl of a stand mixer fitted with the paddle attachment, beat together the butter and coconut milk on medium speed until smooth, about 2 minutes. Add the confectioners' sugar, vanilla and coconut extracts, and salt, raise the speed to medium-high, and beat until combined, about 1 minute, stopping the mixer to scrape down the sides of the bowl as needed.

MAKES ENOUGH FOR ONE 8-INCH (20-CM) 3-LAYER CAKE

1 cup (8 oz/250 g) unsalted butter, at room temperature

½ cup (125 ml) coconut milk

4 cups (1 lb/500 g) confectioners' sugar

½ teaspoon pure vanilla extract

½ teaspoon coconut extract

⅛ teaspoon teaspoon salt

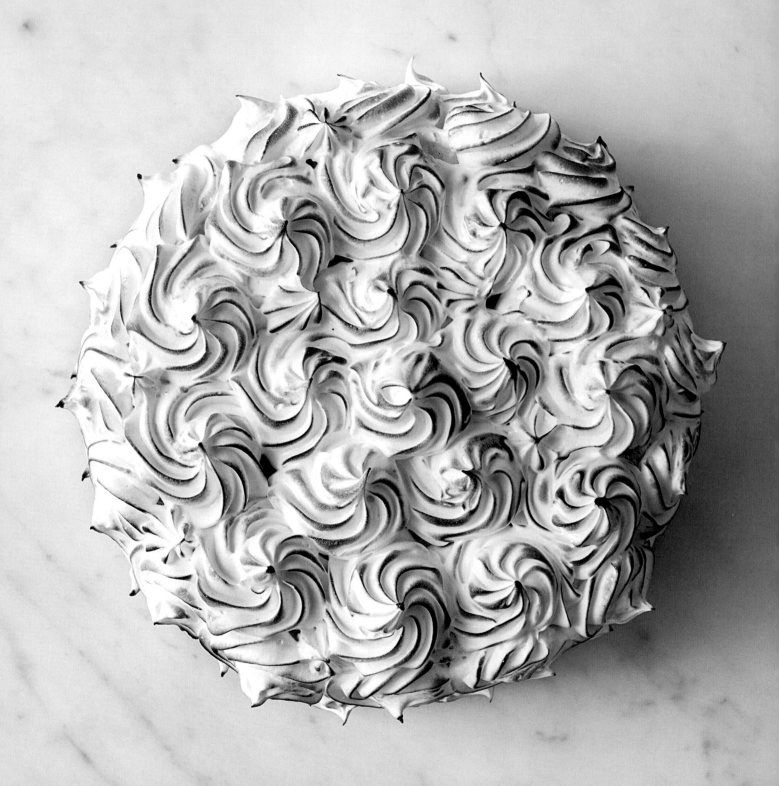

MERINGUE FROSTING

In a saucepan over medium-high heat, stir together the 1⅓ cups (11 oz/345 g) sugar, salt, and ½ cup (125 ml) water and cook until a candy thermometer registers 240°F (115°C).

In the bowl of a stand mixer fitted with the whisk attachment, beat together the egg whites and cream of tartar on medium speed until the mixture is foamy. Slowly add the 2 tablespoons sugar, raise the speed to medium-high, and beat until medium-firm peaks form. Reduce the speed to medium and slowly pour in the hot sugar mixture, then raise the speed to high and beat until a thick, glossy meringue forms, about 4 minutes. Add the vanilla and beat for 1 minute.

MAKES ENOUGH FOR ONE ROUND LAYER CAKE

1⅓ cups (11 oz/345 g) plus 2 tablespoons sugar

¼ teaspoon kosher salt

6 large egg whites

½ teaspoon cream of tartar

1 teaspoon pure vanilla extract

CREAM CHEESE FROSTING

In the bowl of a stand mixer fitted with the paddle attachment, beat the butter on medium speed until smooth, about 1 minute. Reduce the speed to low, add the confectioners' sugar, and beat until combined, stopping the mixer to scrape down the sides of the bowl as needed. Add the salt and vanilla and raise the speed to medium-high. Add the cream cheese about 1 tablespoon at a time until combined and no bits of cream cheese remain, about 2 minutes. Raise the speed to high, add the cream, and beat until combined, 30–45 seconds.

MAKES ENOUGH FOR ONE ROUND LAYER CAKE OR 24 CUPCAKES

1 cup (8 oz/250 g) unsalted butter, at room temperature

3 cups (12 oz/375 g) confectioners' sugar

½ teaspoon kosher salt

1 teaspoon pure vanilla extract

1 lb (500 g) cold cream cheese

2 tablespoons heavy cream

WHIPPED CREAM

In the bowl of a stand mixer fitted with the whisk attachment, beat together the cream, granulated sugar, and vanilla on medium-high speed until soft peaks form, about 3 minutes. Use right away, or cover and refrigerate for up to 2 hours.

VARIATION
To make Frangelico Whipped Cream, add 2 tablespoons Frangelico in place of the vanilla extract.

MAKES ABOUT 2 CUPS (310 G)

1 cup (250 ml) heavy cream

¼ cup (2 oz/60 g) granulated sugar

1 teaspoon pure vanilla extract

TECHNIQUES

From decorating sugar cookies to preparing the perfect piecrust, mastering the fundamentals of baking sets the stage for whipping up masterpieces that are sure to impress. Supercharge your creativity and ensure your success with these key techniques.

COOKIE DECORATING PRIMER

While making cookie dough is a science, decorating cookies is definitely an art! So let your creative side shine through (perhaps with a little luster dust), and use our guide to help inspire your masterful creations.

ROYAL ICING

It all begins with royal icing. This stiff white icing, made from confectioners' sugar and egg whites or meringue powder, got its name after it was used to ice Queen Victoria's white wedding cake celebrating her marriage to Prince Albert in 1840.

EQUIPMENT

A pastry bag (made from cloth or sturdy plastic) with an assortment of removable tips ranging in sizes, a silicone spatula, and a small offset spatula will make easy work of decorating.

FOOD COLORING

Liquids, powders, and gels are all used to tint icings and frostings. Gel food coloring is the most concentrated and therefore creates colors that are more vibrant. Also, it won't thin the icing as much as liquid food coloring, which yields colors that are more pastel-toned. You can use a toothpick to add gel food coloring into the icing bit by bit until you are happy with the color. Start light—a little gel goes a long way, and it is easier to add more coloring than it is to lighten up a dark icing.

FILLING A PASTRY BAG

Piping tips for pastry bags are available in a variety of sizes and shapes (most common are plain and fluted). The smaller the number, the smaller the hole, but numbering systems vary slightly by brand.

To fill the pastry bag, firmly push the desired decorating tip down into the small hole in the pastry bag. If you're using a device called a coupler to hold the tip in place, screw it on tightly. Next, form a cuff by folding down the top one-third of the bag. Place one hand under the cuff. Using a silicone spatula, scoop icing into the bag with the other hand to no more than half full. Then unfold the cuff and push the icing down toward the tip, forcing out any air bubbles, and twist the bag closed where the icing ends. With your dominant hand, hold the bag where you just made the twist. With your nondominant hand, hold the bag near the tip, to help stabilize it, and proceed to pipe.

PIPING & FLOODING

Bakers use terms like "piping" and "flooding" when giving instructions for decorating cookies. Piping creates an outline at the edge of the cookie and flooding fills in the outline with icing. You can use the same bowl of white or colored royal icing for both. Scoop out about one-third of the icing into a piping bag for piping, and thin the remaining icing slightly for flooding.

- **To pipe:** Fit your desired tip into a pastry bag and then fill it with royal icing. Pipe a line of icing as close to the edge of the cookie as possible. Let the outline dry for a few minutes before you begin flooding. Or, skip the flooding and just use the piping bag and some decorations to create your finished design.

- **To flood:** Thin the royal icing slightly by adding warm water 1 teaspoon at a time until it is just spreadable but not runny. Then use an offset spatula, a small paintbrush, or the back of a spoon to spread enough icing over the cookie to cover it generously. Check the icing for air bubbles and pop any with a toothpick. Let the cookies dry completely before storing or packaging.

DECORATIONS

There are endless choices for decorations, enough to make every cookie unique. A sprinkling of sanding sugar (also called colored sugar crystals) is a simple way to make cookies sparkle, and rainbow nonpareils lend playfulness to any design. Dragées—tiny beads commonly available in silver, gold, and other metallic hues—add instant glamour to any cookie. Luster dust gives a metallic sheen to your icing; mix the powder with a flavoring extract and apply it with a small, clean paintbrush.

CAKE TIPS & TECHNIQUES

Creating a showstopping cake starts with making sure it bakes correctly and comes out of the pan without a hitch. Here are prepping, mixing, and piping techniques every baker should know.

CUTTING PARCHMENT ROUNDS

To line a cake pan with parchment paper, tear off a piece of parchment paper that is slightly larger than the pan's diameter. Place the cake pan right side up on the parchment and use a pencil to trace the pan's circumference onto the paper. Cut out the circle just slightly inside the traced circle (or square) so that the parchment fits snugly in the pan and doesn't fold up the pan's sides. If you're using several pans, make one for each pan.

GREASING A CAKE PAN

If your recipe calls for buttering and flouring your cake pan, make sure you prep the pan before you make the batter. Unless noted otherwise, cake pans may be prepared as follows:

- To grease the pan, spread about ½ tablespoon unsalted butter into a thin even layer all over the inside of the pan or coat with a thin layer of cooking spray.

- Line the bottom of the pan with a parchment round (see above) and lightly butter the top of the parchment.

- Add 1 tablespoon flour to the pan and, holding the pan over your work surface, rotate the pan so that the flour sticks to the butter all over the inside of the pan.

- Tap the pan, bottom side up, on the work surface to dislodge any excess flour and use the excess in a second pan or discard.

FOLDING IN INGREDIENTS

To fold whipped egg whites (or whipped cream) into a batter, you want to retain as much aeration as possible, so use a gentle hand and as few strokes as possible. With a large rubber spatula, dollop a scoop of the whipped egg whites onto the batter, then gently stir it in; this step lightens the batter to make it easier for folding. Spoon the remaining egg whites onto the batter. Starting in the center of the bowl, use the rubber spatula to "slice" through the whites and batter to the bottom of the bowl, then pull the spatula up the side of the bowl and swoop over the top and back to the middle. This action will gently mix the egg whites and batter together. Continue with this motion, rotating the bowl, until the mixture is combined and no white streaks are visible, being careful not to overmix and lose the aeration.

ASSEMBLING CAKE LAYERS

Removing the cake from the pan:

- Let the cake cool in the pan on a wire rack for about 10 minutes before removing it; this will help prevent the cake from sticking to the pan.

- If making a cake in an ungreased pan (such as chiffon or genoise), run a thin paring knife around the inside edge to release the cake.

- Place the wire rack upside down over the cake pan and invert the rack and pan together. Carefully remove the pan and any parchment lining. Repeat with the remaining cake layer(s). Let the cakes cool completely before proceeding.

Slicing a cake into layers:

- Place the cooled cake on a flat surface; a revolving cake-decorating stand is ideal.

- Hold a ruler up to the side of the cake and mark the midpoint (or where you'd like to slice it) with toothpicks at regular intervals around the cake.

- Using a long serrated knife and a sawing motion, slowly cut the cake where it is marked, rotating the cake as you cut and working your way to the center of the cake.

- Slide the top layer onto a cardboard cake circle or other flat surface.

FILL THE CAKE LAYERS

- Place the bottom cake layer on a cardboard cake circle atop a work surface or on a revolving cake-decorating stand.

- Using a pastry brush, brush away any crumbs.

- Mound the specifed amount of filling onto the center of the cake, then use an icing spatula to evenly spread the filling to the edges. The type of filling and the thickness of the cake will determine the thickness of the filling layer: jam should be thin, curd and frosting should be thicker. If you want to use a pastry bag to pipe the frosting, see the how-to photos on pages 231.

- Top the filling with the next cake layer, placing it cut side up. Do not spread filling on the top layer unless directed in the recipe.

FROST THE CAKE

Follow these steps when frosting a round or square layer cake.

- Place the filled layer cake on a work surface or on a revolving cake-decorating stand. Using an icing spatula, spread a very thin layer of frosting over the top and sides of the cake. This is called the crumb coat. Refrigerate for about 20 minutes to allow the frosting to firm up. This step will ensure that loose crumbs do not invade your final layer of frosting.

- Place the cake on a serving plate or on a revolving cake-decorating stand. Cut 4 strips of parchment paper and tuck them around the cake bottom to protect the surface from drips.

- Set aside a portion of the frosting for decorating and piping, if desired.

- Using an icing spatula, spread a mound of frosting evenly over the top of the cake. Be careful not to lift the icing spatula directly up or you might tear the cake.

- Using the back of the icing spatula, spread the frosting evenly over the sides of the cake, smoothing it gently.

- If you do encounter crumbs, wipe them away from the frosting before adding more frosting to the cake.

- Dip the icing spatula in hot water and wipe dry. Hold the spatula parallel to the side of the cake and smooth the frosting around the entire cake. Wipe the spatula clean, then rewarm it in the water and wipe dry.

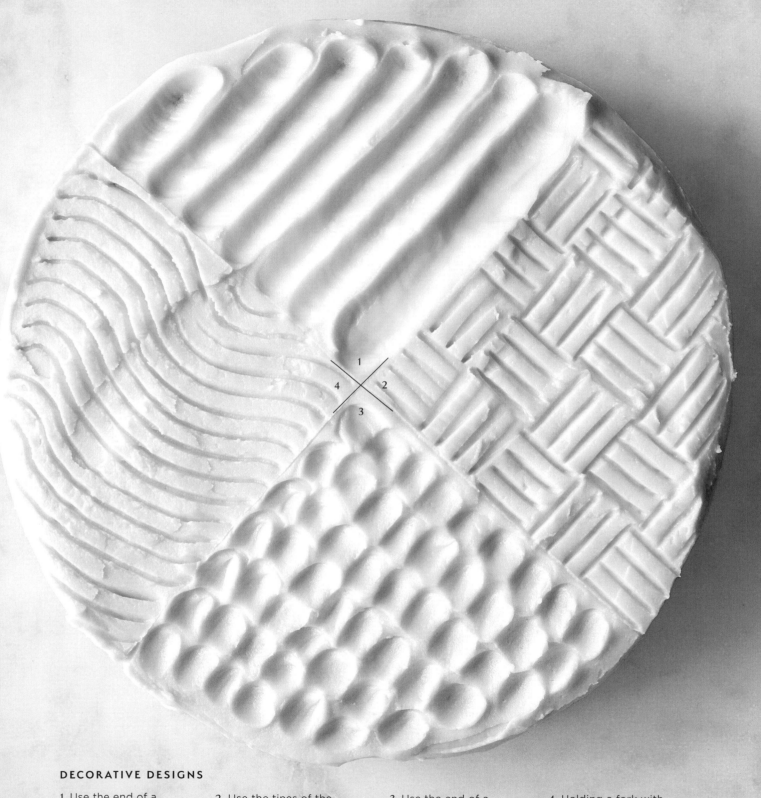

DECORATIVE DESIGNS

1 Use the end of a wooden spoon to draw lines through the buttercream.

2 Use the tines of the back of a fork to create a basket-weave pattern. Start in the center and turn the fork 45 degrees each time you press it into the frosting.

3 Use the end of a wooden spoon to press a pattern into the cake.

4 Holding a fork with the tines pointing straight down, use the tines to draw squiggly lines through the buttercream.

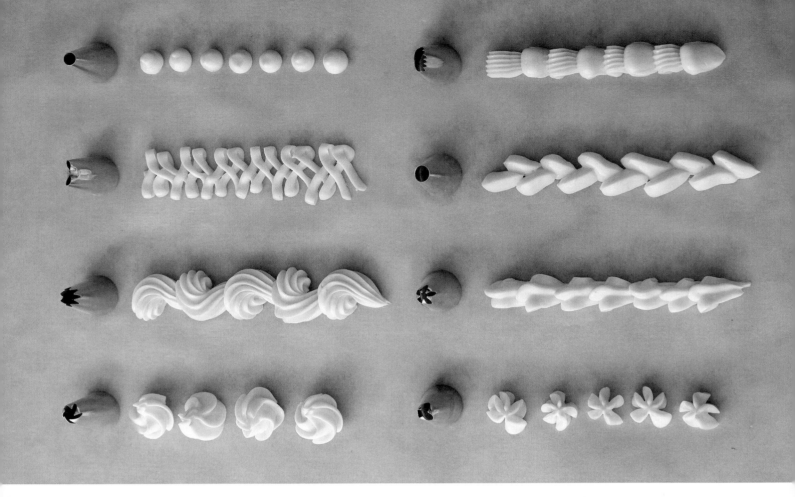

- Hold the spatula parallel to the top of the cake and swipe it across the top from the edge to smooth the edges, while rotating the cake.

- The cake is now ready to be piped with frosting and decorated as desired.

- When you have finished frosting and decorating the cake, remove the parchment strips.

TO MAKE A "NAKED" CAKE

- Be sure to grease your cake pans well to keep your layers neat. Use a pastry brush to brush away any crumbs as you work.

- Stack and fill your cake layers with frosting, using a piping bag to pipe the frosting neatly around the edges.

- Chill the filled layer cake until the frosting hardens. You can then frost the top and add decorations, or take it a step further.

- Spread a layer of frosting over the top, then spread a thin layer down the sides. Use the edge of a metal frosting spatula, an offset spatula, or a metal bench scraper to scrape away enough of the frosting so that you can see the cake layers underneath. Chill until the frosting hardens, then decorate the top.

STORING CAKES

To store an uncut and unfrosted cake, wrap the cake tightly in plastic wrap so that the plastic is touching the top, sides, and bottom. The cake can be stored at room temperature for 2–3 days.

To store a frosted but uncut cake, cover the cake with a cake dome or a large bowl and store at room temperature for 2–3 days.

To store a frosted and cut cake, press a piece of plastic wrap against the cut area, then cover with a cake dome or large bowl and store at room temperature for 2–3 days.

HOW TO FROST A LAYER CAKE

1 Use a pastry bag fitted with a large round tip to pipe
   a border around the edge of the first cake layer.

2 Fill in the center of the layer using a zigzag pattern.

3 Use a small offset spatula to spread the filling over the first cake layer.

4 Add the next layer to the top of the cake.

5 Pipe a border around the edge of the second cake layer.

6 Repeat the process of piping and spreading the filling over the center of the second layer.

7 Add the third layer to the top of the cake.

8 Use a large offset spatula to create a crumb coat around the outside of the cake.

ROLLING OUT PIE DOUGH

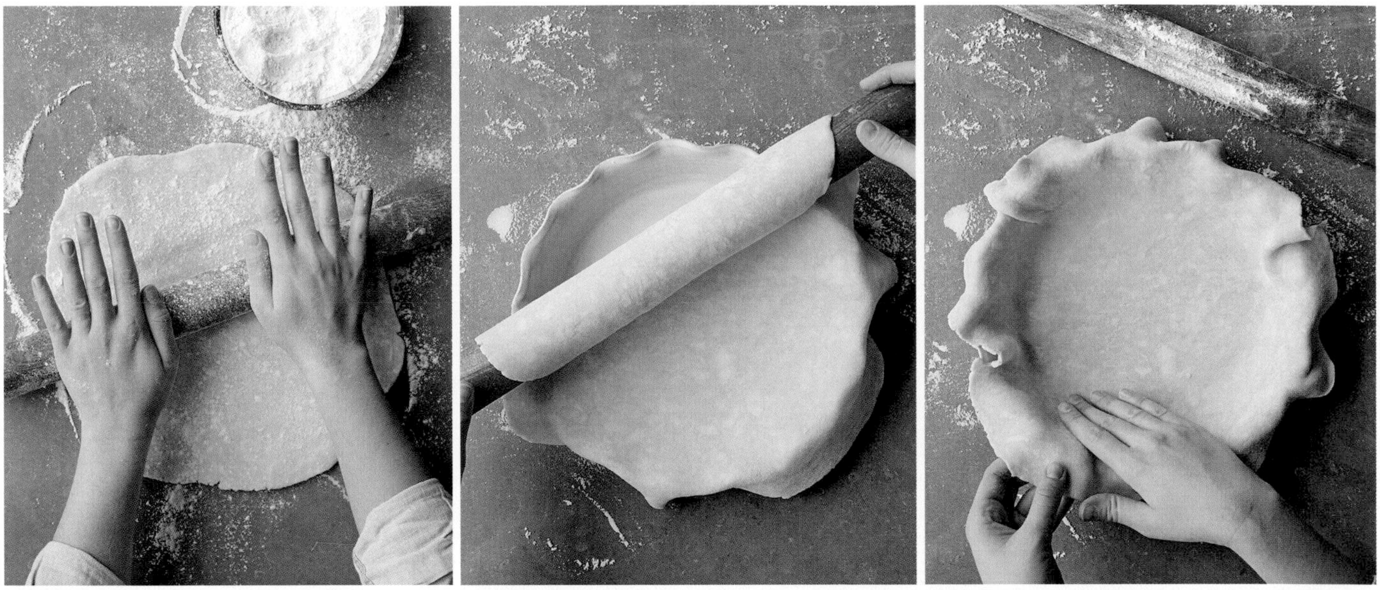

FLUTING PIE DOUGH

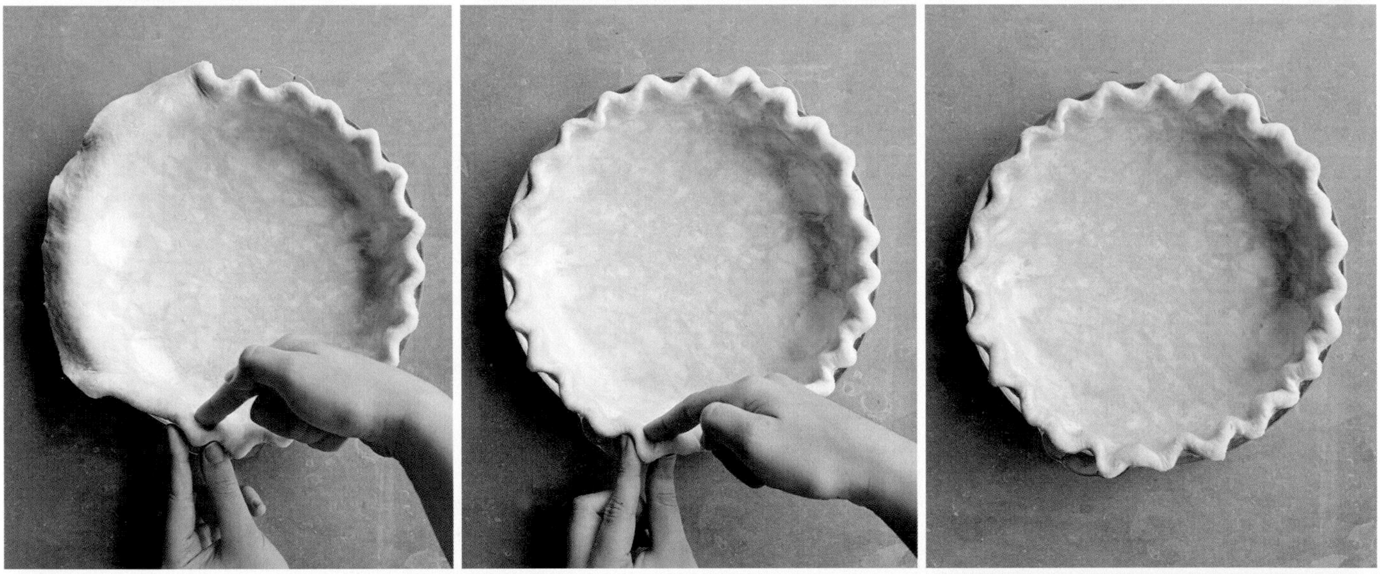

CRIMPING PIE DOUGH

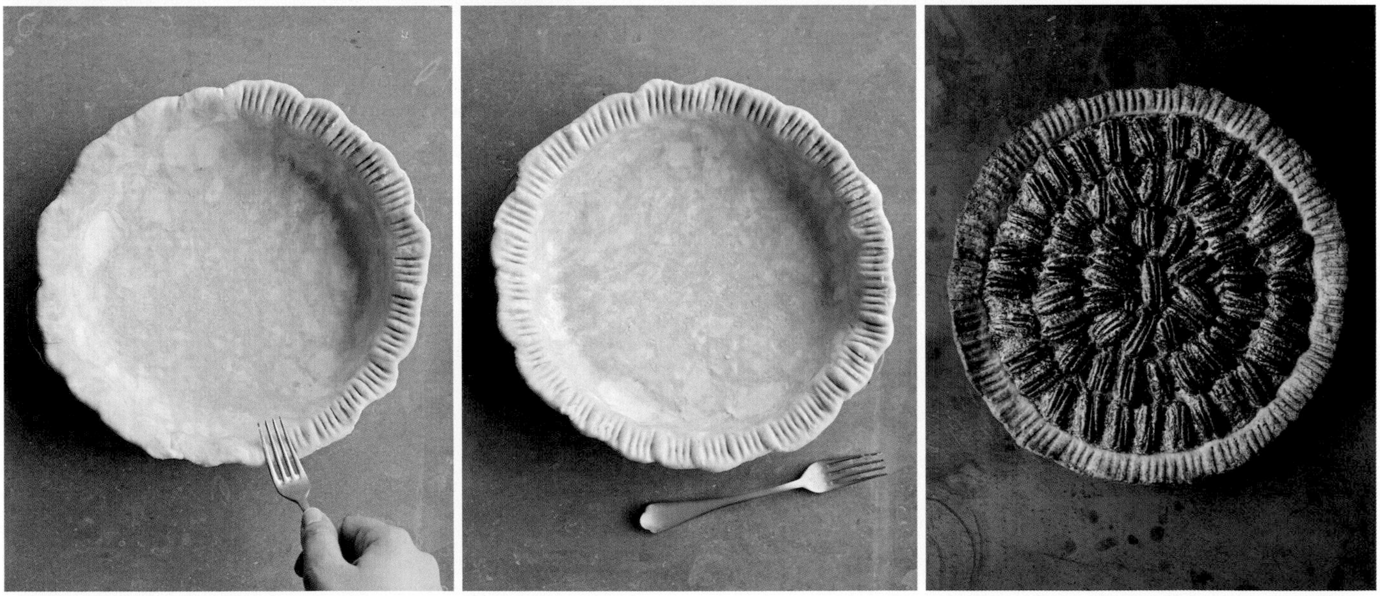

PIES TIPS & TECHNIQUES

Making a great pie starts with the dough. In order to achieve a tender, flaky, and flavorful crust, it's important to not develop the gluten in the dough or you'll wind up with a flat, tough crust. What's the secret? Keep your ingredients cold and don't overwork the dough. Here are more tried-and-true tips to guarantee success every time.

ROLLING OUT PIE DOUGH

Remove the chilled dough disk from the refrigerator. If the dough is too cold and firm to roll out, let it stand at room temperature for about 10 minutes (or less if it's a really warm day). Dust a flat work surface and a rolling pin with flour, then place the dough disk in the center of the work surface.

Starting from the center and rolling toward the edges in all directions, roll out the dough into a round. For a 9-inch (23-cm) pie, roll it out to about 12 inches (30 cm) in diameter and about ⅛ inch (3 mm) thick. Use firm pressure and work quickly to prevent the dough from becoming too warm. If it starts to get overly warm, carefully place it on a baking sheet and refrigerate for a few minutes.

As you roll, lift and rotate the dough several times to make sure it doesn't stick to the work surface, dusting the surface and the rolling pin with flour as needed. Flip the disk over occasionally, especially when you first start, as this helps to keep the dough smooth. If the dough does stick, carefully loosen it with a dough scraper, lightly flour the work surface, and continue to roll. Don't worry if it tears slightly; just press it back together and keep rolling.

LINING A PIE DISH WITH DOUGH

Gently roll the dough loosely around the rolling pin and then unroll it over the pie dish, roughly centering it. Lift the edges to allow the dough to settle evenly into the bottom and sides of the dish, being careful not to stretch or tear the dough. Then trim the edges, leaving a 1-inch (2.5-cm) overhang.

FLUTING OR CRIMPING PIE DOUGH

Whether you make a single-crust, double-crust, or lattice pie, you need to create a finished edge to help the crust stay in place during baking and to give your pie a professional look.

To flute, hold your index finger and thumb about 1 inch (2.5 cm) apart and press them against the outer edge of the pastry rim while pressing with your other index finger from the inside edge of the rim. Repeat all along the rim at 1-inch (2.5-cm) intervals.

To crimp, use the tines of a fork to seal the dough around the edge of the pastry rim.

PREBAKING A SINGLE CRUST

With certain pies, you need to partially or fully bake the pie shell before filling it: when a single-crust pie has a filling that might not bake as long as the piecrust (as with custard pies), and when a pie has a cooked filling and the pie will not return to the oven.

First, roll out the dough and line and crimp the pie shell, then place it in the freezer until hard, about 30 minutes. This will help the pie shell retain its shape when prebaking. Line the inside of the frozen shell with aluminum foil and fill with pie weights (see page 12) before placing in the oven. The weights help prevent the pie from losing its shape or shrinking during baking.

For a partially baked crust, remove it from the oven when it is lightly browned on the edges and the bottom looks dry. For a fully baked crust, bake until the crust is cooked through and golden brown. Let the crust cool completely before adding the filling.

MAKING A CLASSIC LATTICE CRUST

A lattice-topped pie is a double-crust pie with a top woven from strips of dough, usually used with fruit pies. First, roll out and line the pie dish with one dough round. Do not trim the overhang. Fill the pie as directed in your recipe, then roll out the second dough disk so that it is large enough to cover the entire pie, ideally with about a 1-inch (2.5-cm) overhang. Using a ruler as a guide, cut as many dough strips as you can, each 1 inch (2.5 cm) wide.

Lay half of the strips on top of the filled pie, spacing them evenly apart and leaving some space between them. Fold back every other strip halfway and lay down a strip perpendicular across the unfolded strips, then unfold the strips back into place. Fold back the alternate strips, and repeat to lay down a strip perpendicular. Repeat to place the remaining strips of dough evenly across the top, folding back the alternate strips each time. Roll together the ends of the lattice strips and the overhanging edge of the bottom crust so that they sit atop the rim of the pie dish. Flute or crimp the edge (see page 232). Brush the lattice crust with egg mixture and sprinkle with turbinado sugar, if desired.

MAKING A MODERN LATTICE CRUST (THICK AND THIN LATTICE STRIPS)

Follow the directions for creating a classic lattice crust, but cut half of the strips about 2 inches (5 cm) wide and the other half about ¾ inch (2 cm) wide. Weave the lattice together, alternating between the thick and thin strips, and finish as directed.

MAKING A THICK LATTICE CRUST

Follow the directions for creating a classic lattice crust, but cut all of the strips about 1½ inches (4 cm) wide. Lay the strips on the pie as directed so they are nearly touching. Weave the lattice together and finish as directed.

MAKING BRAIDED DOUGH STRIPS

You can use braided dough strips as part of a lattice crust or to decorate the edges of a pie. Roll out a round of pie dough so that it is large enough to cover your pie. Using a ruler as a guide, cut three strips of dough, each about ¼ inch (6 mm) wide. Braid the strips together, pinching the pieces at each end to secure them. Repeat until you have three or four braided strips. Roll out another dough round and line the pie dish, add the filling, and trim the overhang evenly with the rim of the pie dish. Brush the edge of the dough with egg mixture, then lay the braided strips around the rim, pressing them into the edge of the dough. Trim as needed. If using a braid in the lattice, substitute one or two lattice strips with a braid and form the lattice pattern.

PREPARING A DOUBLE-CRUST PIE

A double-crust pie is a pie shell that is filled and then topped with a second round of dough. First, roll out and line the pie dish with one dough round. Do not trim the overhang. Fill the pie as directed in your recipe (usually a fruit filling), then roll out the second dough disk so that it is large enough to cover the entire pie, ideally with about a 1-inch (2.5-cm) overhang. Trim the bottom and top crusts together so they are even. Roll the dough underneath itself so that it sits atop the rim of the pie dish, then flute or crimp the edge (see page 232). Brush the top of the dough with egg mixture and sprinkle with turbinado sugar, if desired.

INDEX

BAKING FAVORITES

Conceived and produced by Weldon Owen International
in collaboration with Williams Sonoma, Inc.
3250 Van Ness Avenue, San Francisco, CA 94109

A WELDON OWEN PRODUCTION

PO Box 3088
San Rafael, CA 94912
www.weldonowen.com

Copyright ©2020 Weldon Owen
and Williams Sonoma, Inc.
All rights reserved, including the right of
reproduction in whole or in part in any form.

Printed in China
10 9 8 7 6 5 4 3 2 1

Library of Congress
Cataloging-in-Publication data is available.

ISBN: 978-1-68188-603-9

WELDON OWEN INTERNATIONAL

CEO Raoul Goff
Publisher Roger Shaw
Associate Publisher Amy Marr
Editorial Assistant Jourdan Plautz
Creative Director Chrissy Kwasnik
Designer Megan Sinead Harris
Managing Editor Lauren LePera
Production Manager Binh Au

Photographer Erin Scott
Food Stylist Lillian Kang
Porp Stylist Claire Mack

Photography on pages 78, 81, 82, 85, 88,
91, 92, 95, 96, 102, 105, 106, 111, 112, 208,
218, 221, 224, and 229–231 by Sang An

Photography on pages 9, 10, 13, 16, 68, 118,
121, 122, 125, 126, 129, 130, 133, 134, 137, 138,
141, 142, 145, 146, 151, 152, 158, 161, 162, 165,
166, 212, 232, 235, and 240 by Eva Kolenko

Photography on pages 23, 24, 27, 28, 31,
32, 36, 39, 43, 44, 47, 48, 54, 57, 58, 61, 71,
72, 77, 211, and 227 by Annabelle Breakey

Photography on pages 62, 67, 115, and 179
by Aubrie Pick

Weldon Owen wishes to thank the following people
for their generous support in producing this book:
Kris Balloun, Lesley Bruynesteyn, Inkan Chrisman, Amanda Fredrickson,
Josephine Hsu, Glenn Jenkins, Shelly Kaldunski, Natasha Kolenko, Kim Laidlaw,
Emily McFarren, Alessandra Motorola, Elizabeth Parson, and Jen Straus.